PARTNERSHIP

WILLIAM TAYLOR

William Taylor's Partnership is a lively, brilliant and courageous exposition of Paul's Letter to the Philippians. I am delighted to recommend this gem of a book about a gem of a New Testament church. It is the work of a first class preacher of God's Word and deserves to be very widely read.

Rev Dr Mark Stibbe

You will this book on Philippians exudes the warmth of the letter itself. It is a faithful explanation of the letter, engages with our lives and is insightfully applied.

William is one of the finest leaders I know. His background as a Captain in the Royal Greenjackets prepared him well for leadership in the church. He is a man who recognises the eternal significance of pastoral leadership; it is his compassionate pastoral care, so evident at St Helen's, which reflects itself in his preaching and in this book.

I warmly recommend it to you.

David Cook, Sydney Missionary & Bible College

PARTNERSHIP

Concise, portable spiritual food - Philippians

W ILLIAM T AYLOR

ST HELEN'S
MEDIA

CHRISTIAN
FOCUS

Copyright © William Taylor

ISBN 1-84550-231-0
ISBN 978-1-84550-231-7

10 9 8 7 6 5 4 3 2 1

Published in 2007
by
Christian Focus Publications Ltd.,
Geanies House, Fearn, Tain, Ross-shire,
IV20 1TW, Scotland, UK
www.christianfocus.com
with
St Helen's Media,
Great St Helen's, London
EC3A 6AT, England, UK
www.st-helens.org.uk

Cover design by Moose77.com

Printed and bound by
Nørhaven Paperback A/S, Denmark

Contents

About the Author

William Taylor served in the British Army from 1983-88. Having studied at Ridley Hall, Cambridge, he was ordained in 1991 and subsequently appointed curate at Christ Church, Bromley. In 1995 he joined St Helen's, Bishopsgate, an historic church in the City of London, where he became Rector in 1998. He is married to Janet, and they have three children - Emily, Digby and Archie.

Preface

It is my deep conviction that God works in His mighty power by His Spirit through His Word. Jesus puts it that way in John 6:63: *It is the Spirit who gives life; the flesh is of no avail. The words that I have spoken to you are spirit and life.* It is by Jesus' life-giving and eternal Word that his people are born again by the Spirit (1 Peter 1:23); it is by Jesus' life-giving Word that His people grow up to maturity in salvation (1 Peter 2:2). When Philip asks to be shown the Father (John 14:8), Jesus' answer is framed in terms of the work of the Spirit in giving us His word through the Apostles' teaching. Any mighty work of the Spirit of God and any expression of genuine Christian discipleship will have at its very centre the living Word of God. The Bible is the essential bread-and-butter of every Christian's life and growth. Scripture is the vital diet of every healthy church and of every authentic movement of the Spirit.

The aim of this book is to help bring the Word of God to the people of God through the simple expounding of that Word. It is my desire that Christian people will be strengthened in their discipleship and encouraged to engage in bold and adventurous gospel partnership through this exposition of Paul's letter to the Philippians. The book originated from a series of talks given at St Helen's and then within the Tuesday lunchtime ministry to business people in the City of London. It is an immense privilege to serve God within a church family that is hungry to be taught God's Word, and many of the reflections and discoveries in this book come as a result of conversations and observations made by members of the church family as we have explored the letter together. As with any Bible teaching enterprise, it is very much a 'work in progress'.

Alongside a close study of the text of Philippians I have found a number of commentaries and books particularly helpful. Amongst the most useful have been the following: Peter O'Brien, *Commentary on Philippians,* NIGTC, Eerdmans; J. A. Motyer, *The Message of Philippians,* BST, IVP; Gordon Fee, *Paul's letter to the Philippians,* NICNT, Eerdmans; D. A. Carson, *Basics for Believers*, IVP.

I am enormously grateful to Rachel Meek for her help in editing my transcripts, and to Claire Tunks and Brian O'Donoghue who have painstakingly read and re-read each chapter. Each of them has been gracious enough not to ask the author what on earth he did in all those English lessons at school when he should have been learning the rudimentary principles of spelling and grammar that are so useful in making the English language intelligible!

ONE

The Model Church on Track with God in Gospel Partnership

Philippians 1:1-11

¹ Paul and Timothy, servants of Christ Jesus, To all the saints in Christ Jesus who are at Philippi, with the overseers and deacons: ² Grace to you and peace from God our Father and the Lord Jesus Christ.

³ I thank my God in all my remembrance of you, ⁴ always in every prayer of mine for you all making my prayer with joy, ⁵ because of your partnership in the gospel from the first day until now. ⁶ And I am sure of this, that he who began a good work in you will bring it to completion at the day of Jesus Christ. ⁷ It is right for me to feel this way about you all, because I hold you in my heart, for you are all partakers with me of grace, both in my imprisonment and in the defence and confirmation of the gospel. ⁸ For God is my witness, how I yearn for you all with the affection of Christ Jesus. ⁹ And it is my prayer that your love may abound more and more, with knowledge and all discernment, ¹⁰ so that you may approve what is excellent, and so be pure and blameless for the day of Christ, ¹¹ filled with the fruit of righteousness that comes through Jesus Christ, to the glory and praise of God.

The churches of Philippi and Thessalonica are in many senses the model churches of the New Testament. Paul wrote of them in 2 Corinthians that *'in a severe test of affliction, their abundance of joy and their extreme poverty have overflowed in a wealth of generosity on their part'* (8:2). So we might say of the church in Philippi that it is a gem of a church. A showcase church.

Paul identifies one or two issues in this church that need to be dealt with, and we shall come to them later. But for now, even in the opening eleven verses of his letter, we can see that Paul regards the church in Philippi as a model church, on track with God. He is full of thanks for them in verse 3: *I thank my God in all my remembrance of you*, and expresses a steady confidence about them in verse 6: *I am sure of this.*

Paul writes to all the Christians in Philippi, expressing his joy and gratitude for every one of them:

Verse 1: *to **all** the saints*

Verse 3–4: *always in every prayer of mine for you **all***

Verse 7: *it is right for me to feel this way about you **all***

Verse 7: *you are **all** partakers with me*

Verse 8: *God is my witness how I yearn for you **all**.*

So here is a gloriously refreshing church where everyone appears to be going well. If this were a report at a shareholders' meeting, we might be asking ourselves whether the chairman really has got this right! Is something being hidden? It seems too good to be true! If this were an assessment of an athlete, we might be asking ourselves whether there has been some performance-enhancing substance in the diet! And if this were an end-of-term report, we might be asking ourselves if the teacher had got the right child!

I was at a parents' evening recently where another parent told me that he had just listened with some amazement to the most glowing report he had ever heard in his life. It was only towards the end of the session with the teacher that they both realized that it was not his child the teacher was speaking about!

However, there's no doubting that Paul has the right church. This is Philippi. Perched on the edge of Southern Greece, it was the first city to hear the Christian message in mainland Europe. Paul is writing to all the Christians there – the word *saint* in the Bible refers to any Christian person. He specifically mentions all the leaders or overseers of the church, but he is joyfully and confidently grateful for every single believer.

Since Philippi is a model church, I would like to suggest that studies in this letter to the Philippians will be wonderfully refreshing for any church or individual Christian to engage in. We often rightly study letters from the New Testament written to correct significant faults in the early church. They help us to identify, correct and guard against similar faults in our own churches. But here in Paul's letter to the Philippians we have a model church. The instruction we are going to receive is almost entirely positive. For this reason, we will be able to hold this letter up as a plumbline against our own church and our own personal discipleship as we ask ourselves: how do we match up? But first, we need to ask where Paul's extraordinary joy and confidence in the Philippian believers comes from.

The joyful confidence of gospel partnership

The answer is given in two ways as Paul explains both the source of his confidence and the ground of his confidence.

Paul is joyfully confident because the church in Philippi is, from start to finish, God's work.

At least three times Paul stresses that God is the **source** of the Philippian church:

Verse 3: *I thank **my God**.*

Verse 6: ***He** who began a good work in you*

Verse 7: *you are all partakers with me **of grace** ...*

In other words, Paul is full of joyful confidence because he is clear that any genuinely Christian work is started, sustained and completed by God, and by God alone.

The phrase *the day of Jesus Christ* refers to the return of Jesus on the Last Day. So in verses 3-6 we get a sense of God's work in the past, in the present and in the future. It is God's work from *the first day*, and *until now,* and on until *completion at the day of Jesus Christ.* God started the church in Philippi. God continues to sustain the church in Philippi. God will bring His work to completion amongst his people in the church at Philippi.

It is worth pondering for a moment this initiating, energizing and completing grace of God. When interrupted by the buzzer, Magnus Magnusson, quizmaster of the TV show Mastermind (a great British institution), always said, 'I've started so I'll finish'. Paul is confident that when God sets out on a project he will not leave it unfinished. God is not like a dodgy builder who departs from a site with parts of the job still left undone. There is no snagging with God.

When He starts a work in a believer's life and in a church family, He ensures that this group of believers will make it through to the great day of the return of Jesus Christ.

I'd like to encourage you to pause here and think about four or five other Christian believers in your church family. Parents, no doubt, will think of children. Youth leaders may think of teenagers. Home group members might consider one another. You might even think about yourself!

God began His good work in each one of His people: it was His initiative. God has brought each one to the point at which they now stand with Him: it was His enabling. God has underwritten His work in the life of each believer with all His divine, creative power and authority. God guarantees to bring each one of them through to the great day of Jesus' return. That is some assurance! And since it is God's work – from start to finish – it is right that we should be filled with grateful praise and thanks to God. Even as I write I find myself challenged to be more thankful to God for His work in the life of His people.

But as we look more closely at verses 1-8 we will see that while the **source** of Paul's joyful confidence is God, the **ground** for his joyful confidence is the Philippians' partnership, which God has enabled.

It is really important that we notice this point, for if we miss it we might end up with a misplaced confidence and a false joy. Of course Paul is clear that the **source** of every believer in Philippi is God's initiating, sustaining and completing grace. But the reason Paul can be so certain that God's grace is at work in the church in Philippi, is that they have remained constant in their gospel partnership with him. It is the partnership of the Philippians, through thick and thin, that has shown them to be a genuine, authentic, model church of God. The Philippian Christians really have been partners with Paul in the grace of God. This is why Paul has confidence that God is at work in them to bring them to completion at the last day.

The word 'partnership' is often translated as 'fellowship'. I'm afraid that when I hear that word fellowship in a Christian context I immediately think of bland meetings where all that happens is a lot of chat and the occasional cringe-worthy chorus, together with cups of rather gruesome coffee, sausage rolls and quiches.

Nothing could be further from the New Testament idea of fellowship or partnership. The word comes from the business arena, so business men and women will understand precisely what is being spoken about here. Partnership involves energetic, wholehearted, active and consistent engagement in a project. The word could be used of a mergers and acquisitions team, as they stay up all night sweating away at their computer screens in pursuit of that dream deal. It could be used of a team member on the sports field, as he or she engages with other members of the team to achieve a common goal – think for instance of the English rugby XV or of your national football team.

So Paul isn't speaking about a cosy Christian club, is he? Nor is he speaking about an occasional interest shown in Christian things out of a sense of duty. This is not 'one hour a week' religion, nor that once-a-year act of mowing the Church grass to help God out and keep God's show on the road. No! Verse 7 puts it plainly: *you are all partakers with me of grace both in my imprisonment and in the defence and confirmation of the gospel.*

Paul is *right* to have every confidence in and gratitude for the work of God in every member of the Philippian church, *for* every one of them has proved to be God's man or God's woman as God has enabled them, by His grace, to engage with Paul in gospel work. They have been active partners, both in their support of him as he is imprisoned and in the ongoing work of defending and confirming the gospel through their proclamation. All of them have been involved. He writes to *all the saints*. It is the work of every individual in the church, acting together. Therefore, while the **source** of Paul's joyful confidence is God, the **grounds** for Paul's joyful confidence is the partnership of these believers through thick and thin, which God has enabled.

Paul has been **imprisoned** for preaching about Jesus, and we'll see a great deal more about this later in the letter. The Philippians could have backed away from their partnership with Paul. After all, they were Roman citizens. To stand with Paul would have put their reputations at risk. Despite the risks, they stood with Paul.

Paul has **defended** the truth about Jesus in the public domain. He was dragged into the market place at Philippi. There, in the presence of the local magistrates, he was forced to give a defence of what he was preaching. This was the equivalent of trial by media. The Philippians could have backed off. They must have been tempted to distance themselves from him: 'well, you know, that's not quite my kind of Christianity.... We don't go in for that brand here in our church.' Yet they stood with Paul.

Paul has **confirmed** the truth about Jesus by showing to emperors, governors and religious leaders the evidence for the gospel, that Jesus Christ is God's anointed king and universal Lord of all humanity. He has used the Old Testament to prove his point. He has pointed them to the witnesses of the resurrection of Jesus who could bear witness to the truth of his words. He has argued in public and in private, through spoken word and through written word, in person and through envoy. The Philippians could have backed off: 'We'll leave that to Paul ... he's the extrovert ... he's the one who is into that sort of thing. Let Paul talk the talk, we'll carry on quietly walking the walk.' Nevertheless, they stood with Paul!

So here is an entire church that is energetically, actively, wholeheartedly, consistently, persistently showing themselves to be in active partnership. And that gives Paul joyful gratitude and immense confidence.

This is God's work – He began it!

This is God's work – He is continuing it!

This is God's work – He'll complete it!

This is God's work – praise Him for it!

This is not a letter for a church that is struggling to stand with Jesus in a particular area. If we want a church like that, we need to go to a letter such as 1 or 2 Corinthians, or Colossians. Those letters are written to churches that are struggling to stick with Jesus and his teaching. They have big problems in areas such as sexuality and sexual behaviour, love, and the issue of how we can know and serve God together. But this isn't a letter for a church like that!

Nor is this a letter for a church that is beginning to develop a bit of spiritual middle-age spread. If we wanted a part of the Bible to address that sort of condition we might go to Hebrews, where the recipients of the letter are tempted to give up and drift away from Jesus.

This is a letter to a church that is really going well. A gem of a church. A showcase church.

The church in Philippi is a church that is prepared to stand with Jesus, to take the flak with Jesus, and to spread the gospel with Jesus. The believers have stuck their heads above the parapet with Jesus, and they have put their reputation on the line with Jesus. Chapter 3 of this book shows that they have been ready to be vilified in public with Paul and to suffer with Paul as he has proclaimed the gospel of Jesus Christ as Lord.

And Paul says that, to the extent that we have been concerned to be partners with him in such ways, whether as individual believers or as churches, we ought also to be greatly encouraged, filled with joy, and confident for the future. For such participation is evidence that God has begun a work in us. And the fact that we are keeping on going, fully engaged in the work of the gospel, together with Paul, should fill us with glad and joyful confidence that we are on track with God.

I wonder, when was the last time that we joined with Paul and engaged in the kind of overflowing gratitude and praise to God for Christians, either in our own church or around the world, who have been genuine partners in authentic gospel ministry? As I write I can think of church families with whom the church in which I serve has contact, in London and right across Britain, in Latvia, in Cape Town, in Durban and Johannesburg, in Sydney and Melbourne, in Paris, in Brussels, and in the United States of America. Often it is all too easy to spot the faults and problems in churches. But Paul overflows with grateful confidence to God for God's initiating, sustaining and completing grace in His people.

But what about our own church? If we belong to a church like this – one that is unashamedly engaged in the defence and confirmation of the gospel of Jesus Christ our Lord – then we should be deeply grateful to God, full of joy, and confidently assured that what is going on in our church is indeed God's work. He has started so He will finish!

But this joyful confidence leaves us asking the question ... what does Paul want for a church like this?

Paul's heartfelt longing on behalf of the Philippians

In verses 9-11 Paul appears to have just one thing in mind. He has the end in sight:

> And it is my prayer that your love may abound more and more, with knowledge and all discernment, so that you may approve what is excellent, and so be pure and blameless for the day of Christ, filled with the fruit of righteousness that comes through Jesus Christ, to the glory and praise of God.

This is the second time Paul has mentioned *the day of Christ*. It refers to the day of Jesus' glorious return as Lord of heaven and earth, when *every knee will bow, in heaven and on earth, and under the earth, and every tongue confess that Jesus Christ is Lord, to the glory of God the Father* (2:10-11). On that day our *Saviour, the Lord Jesus Christ ... will transform our lowly body to be like his glorious body by the power that enables him even to subject all things to himself* (3:20-2). Back in verse 6, Paul told us that he is sure God will bring the Philippians to that great day. Now he is eager that on that great day when Jesus returns, the Philippians will be *filled with the fruit of righteousness that comes through Jesus Christ to the glory and praise of God* (v. 11). This is an image from late autumn. It is a picture of a bumper harvest.

For someone like myself who grew up on a working farm in Cornwall, this image could not be more evocative. Any one-time farmers will have vivid memories of riding in on top of the grain or straw trailers. But we don't have to be familiar with the realities of Constable's painting 'The Haywain' to get the idea. After all, the teacher longs for a fruitful harvest when the final crop of exam results comes in; the accountant looks for the fruitful harvest of a successful audit; the analyst lives for the fruitful harvest of a set of outstanding end-of-year figures.

Paul sees that the end has not yet come. His eyes are fixed on the future and he longs to maximize the praise and glory of Jesus on that day. So, his great desire for the model church is that the fruits of partnership in gospel ministry should go on abounding, and that on the great day of Christ, when He returns in glory to usher in His new heaven and new earth, the members of this model church will be filled to overflowing with the fruit of righteousness, to the glory of Jesus.

After all that the Philippians have been through with Paul we might expect him to say: 'Look, Philippians,

I'm just hoping that you might manage a spot of rest and recuperation. Why not take a couple of years off from standing with me in the abuse and suffering that come from defending and proclaiming the gospel.' But he doesn't!

Instead, Paul's great desire is that they, together with all believers, make it to the end of the Christian life – to the day of Christ Jesus. He longs that on the Great Day of Christ we draw in, if you like, at the seat of our Massey-Ferguson (that's a type of tractor, by the way!) with a vast trailer towed behind, filled with the fruit that comes from God having made us righteous (3:9).

As I have thought about this picture, I have to say it has set me wondering. Where will the resources come from to keep the Philippians on track to the end? How much can the Philippians go on taking? They have given, and given, and given, and given. Remember Paul's comment back in 2 Corinthians: *they gave beyond their means, of their own free will, begging us earnestly for the favour of taking part ...*(8:3-4).

So where will the resources come from to produce such a bumper harvest? In brief, the answer is there already for us in verse 11. *The fruit of righteousness* is the fruit that comes from having been brought into a right relationship with God and thus being enabled to live lives of pure, blameless and selfless service (there will be much more on this in 3:7-11). But the idea begins in verse 8 which, while it sits grammatically with verses 3-7, is at the same time part of the foundation for verse 9: *For God is my witness how I yearn for you all with the affection of Christ Jesus. And it is my prayer that your love may abound more and more, with knowledge and all discernment.*

Do you see the logic? Paul longs for and yearns for the Philippians *with all the affection of* Christ. He has been given by God a Christ-like love and affection for them. The word *affection* is one that speaks of something deep within. The word literally means 'inward parts' or 'entrails'! Paul has an affectionate longing for the Philippians that comes from deep down. It's not a natural thing. It comes from within and it is planted there by Jesus. When Paul became a Christian, he came to grasp the love of Christ for himself and for everyone else. Now he has this unique, exclusively Christian, loving compassion for God's work and for God's people.

He's not simply talking about an occasional decent deed. It's not a gooey, Hollywood, soupy sentimentalism which is there in the good times but evaporates when the going gets tough. Paul now finds himself reaching out to the Philippians with the selfless, self-sacrificial love of Christ that we see demonstrated on the cross.

Later in this letter Paul is going to expand on the love of Jesus in considerable detail (2:5-11). He will also talk quite bluntly to the Philippians about how Jesus' love should shape their behaviour towards one another (2:1-4; 4:2-4). For now, however, Paul's prayer is that this well of the love of Christ, that has been placed within each believer, will increase and overflow out of his gospel partners in Philippi. His prayer is that this love will be marked by a deep personal *knowledge* of God's character, together with practical *discernment*, so that they can test and approve what is excellent and pleasing to God in every decision. The *knowledge* in verse 9 speaks of a relational knowing of someone; it is not a mere intellectualism. The *discernment* in verse 9 speaks of that ability to know almost instinctively what it is that will please and delight someone which can only come from knowing them deeply. To *approve what is excellent* in verse 10 speaks of making decisions that are not just 'good', but 'the very best'.

So, with an ever-deepening grasp of the love of Christ shaping the lives of the Philippians, they will be able to go on to produce a greater and greater harvest of pure and blameless good deeds to the glory of Christ at His return. All this is *the fruit of righteousness*, because the seed that produces this kind of fruit is the right relationship with God that has been made possible through Jesus' death on the cross.

It is a wonderful picture, isn't it? Every decision, every situation, every relationship governed by a growing abundance of the love of Jesus, with deep personal knowledge of Jesus and understanding of how He would speak and act and direct His energies in each circumstance.

Paul's prayer for the Philippians is that, since they are now in a right relationship with God, Jesus' love for His people will shape their **behaviour** throughout the day – such as how they use their resources, how they spend their time, their energy, their money, their holidays.

Paul's prayer for the Philippians is that, since they are now in a right relationship with God, Jesus' selfless love will shape their every **situation** – such as how they react at work, at rest, at play, at home, in the office, the classroom, on the ward or on the road.

Paul's prayer for the Philippians is that, since they are now in a right relationship with God, Jesus' selfless love will also shape each of their **relationships** – how they respond – whether to their boss, their colleague, their friends or their family.

So then, the first eight verses show us that the model church which is on track with God in gospel partnership has great cause for joyful and confident gratitude to God. Verses 9-11 show us that there is more to look forward to. We have not yet reached the *day of Christ*. Therefore, the model church that is on track with God in gospel partnership still has time for further work to the praise of His glory. All this comes *through Jesus Christ* and it is only as a result of His *love abounding more and more with knowledge and discernment* within His people. It is all a result of *knowing Jesus*: it is *the fruit of righteousness*. He enables and sustains it, but there is still room for an increase in the harvest.

Let's imagine for a moment that we are able to say verses 3-8 are true of our local church. Praise God! We have stood 'shoulder to shoulder' with the teaching and ministry of the apostle Paul. No doubt it will have involved some degree of abuse and suffering, a lot of hard work and considerable personal sacrifice. However, there may come a day when we will tempted to say: 'it is time to hand the baton on to someone else.' Indeed, most of us will probably reach such a point in our lives.

I find myself, after just twenty-seven years as a Christian, sometimes thinking about the possibility of stepping back a little from some of the pressures and stresses of Christian service. It can be personally demanding to be a partner with a 'Paul-shaped' ministry when everyone and everything around us is pointing in the opposite direction.

But *the day of Christ* has not yet arrived. And Paul's prayer for this model church in Philippi is that the lives of its members will be energized by the love of Jesus. He wants all believers to increase and overflow in deeper and deeper personal understanding of Jesus' love. This love of Jesus, flowing from His death on the cross, will enable them to make selfless and sacrificial decisions. The result? A bumper harvest that comes from Him having made His people righteous – to the praise and glory of God!

Questions:

1. Verses 1-8: Why is it that Paul is able to thank God for the church at Philippi?

2. Verses 1-8: What evidence is there in these verses that all is going well?

3. Verses 9-11: Paul prays here for fruit in the Philippians. What is it that will produce this fruit?

4. In what ways is your church exercising the kind of partnership that Paul speaks of here?

5. How do you think these verses should affect our prayers and praise for our own church and for others in this country and overseas with whom we are in partnership?

6. How should these verses change the way we talk to our Christian friends and pray for them?

TWO

The Model Pastor on Track with God in Gospel Proclamation

Philippians 1:12-26

[12] I want you to know, brothers, that what has happened to me has really served to advance the gospel, [13] so that it has become known throughout the whole imperial guard and to all the rest that my imprisonment is for Christ. [14] And most of the brothers, having become confident in the Lord by my imprisonment, are much more bold to speak the word without fear.

[15] Some indeed preach Christ from envy and rivalry, but others from good will. [16] The latter do it out of love, knowing that I am put here for the defence of the gospel. [17] The former proclaim Christ out of rivalry, not sincerely but thinking to afflict me in my imprisonment. [18] What then? Only that in every way, whether in pretence or in truth, Christ is proclaimed, and in that I rejoice.

Yes, and I will rejoice, [19] for I know that through your prayers and the help of the Spirit of Jesus Christ this will turn out for my deliverance, [20] as it is my eager expectation and hope that I will not be at all ashamed, but that with full courage now as always Christ will be honoured in my body, whether by life or by death. [21] For to me to live is Christ, and to die is gain. [22] If I am to live in the flesh, that means fruitful labour for me. Yet which I shall choose I cannot tell.

[23] I am hard pressed between the two. My desire is to depart and be with Christ, for that is far better. [24] But to remain in the flesh is more necessary on your account. [25] Convinced of this, I know that I will remain and continue with you all, for your progress and joy in the faith, [26] so that in me you may have ample cause to glory in Christ Jesus, because of my coming to you again.

Some of us in our misspent youth will have come across the Monty Python film, *The Life of Brian*. It was a deliberately irreverent contribution to the cinema screens of the 1980s. In it was a song that has become almost a part of our early twenty-first-century culture in England – 'Always look on the bright side of life'. It was written as a parody of the Christian's ability to be positive in the face of seemingly overwhelming odds, so perhaps it isn't surprising that it has become a favourite of the English football team's long-suffering fan club. And now, in the light of consistent failure, in the absence of any major trophy for decades, the English football fans sing forlornly: 'Always look on the bright side of life.'

As we look at Philippians 1:12-26 we might be tempted to think that Paul is engaged in a similar exercise of 'hale-and-hearty' self-delusion. After all, Paul is in prison awaiting trial following hostile opposition from outside the Christian community. At the same time he is aware of rivalry from within, amongst the Christians in Rome. Additionally, it is highly possible that the outcome of his trial might be death. This is hardly the brightest of scenarios! Yet Paul seems almost unable to do anything other than 'look on the bright side.'

The reason for Paul's rejoicing is given in verse 18: *What then? Only that in every way, whether in pretence or in truth, Christ is proclaimed, and in that I rejoice.* So Paul's governing concern is for the proclamation of the glorious good news that Jesus Christ is Lord. In any and every circumstance his number-one priority is to proclaim Jesus. This is what causes him joy and gladness, and this is what gives him delight in his heart. As Paul awaits his trial in prison in Rome, he recognizes that God has sovereignly ordered his circumstances so that the good news of Jesus should be proclaimed wherever he finds himself:

Verse 12: *what has happened to me has really served to advance the gospel*

Verse 14: *most of the brothers ... are much more bold to speak the Word without fear*

Verse 18: *... Christ is proclaimed, and in that I rejoice. Yes, and I will rejoice ...'*

Verse 20: *... it is my eager expectation and hope ... that with full courage (outspokenness) Christ will be honoured in my body.*

Verse 25: *convinced of this I will remain and continue with you all for your progress and joy in the faith*

But why is it that Paul feels the need to say all of this to the Philippians? The answer comes from understanding something of the Philippians' own situation. Later in this chapter it becomes evident that the Philippians are *engaged in the same conflict that you saw I had and now hear that I still have* (v. 30). So, in exactly the same way as Paul, the church at Philippi is facing **hostility from outside** the Christian community. Furthermore, there is also some evidence of **rivalry within.** Paul addresses this directly in 2:3: *do* *nothing from rivalry or conceit, but in humility count others more significant than yourselves.*

Once we understand the situation the Philippians are facing, we can see that this part of the letter is tailor-made by Paul in order to encourage his partners in Philippi in the conflict, the rivalry and the temptation to give up that they appear to be facing. Paul's aim is that the Philippians join with him, and see every circumstance and situation in which they find themselves as an opportunity to make the proclamation of Jesus Christ as Lord their first priority. Once they do this, they too will be able to see things from a totally different perspective. They too will 'look on the bright side of life.'

Here then is the **model pastor** showing the **model church** how they should respond to **hostility, rivalry and temptation to backslide.** The number-one priority in any and every circumstance is – you've guessed it – the proclamation of the gospel!

In the face of hostility from without – praise God! The gospel is proclaimed

We can see that Paul understands the hostility he has been facing to have been a good thing, because through it the gospel has been proclaimed to many more people: *I want you to know brothers that what has happened to me has really served to advance the gospel* (v. 12) .

In order to understand what is going on properly, it is necessary to find out a little bit more about the nature of the hostility that Paul is facing. The Philippians are *engaged in the same conflict that you saw **I had** and now hear that **I still*** *have* (1:30), which means that the opposition Paul is currently facing is precisely the same kind of opposition that the Philippians *saw* him facing when Paul was with them in person.

That opposition is described in Acts 16. When Paul first took the gospel to Philippi, a slave girl with the ability to tell people's fortunes was converted. Once converted she stopped her fortune-telling – the gospel brought radical change in her life. The story is taken up in Acts 16:19-22:

> ... when her owners saw that their hope of gain was gone, they seized Paul and Silas and dragged them into the market place before the rulers. And when they had brought them to the magistrates, they said, 'These men are Jews, and they are disturbing our city. They advocate customs that are not lawful for us as Romans to accept or practise.' The crowd joined in attacking them, and the magistrates tore the garments off them and gave orders to beat them with rods.

So, greedy, pagan businessmen in Philippi see the possibility of the gospel reducing their profit margin. They drag Paul into the marketplace and accuse him in front of the establishment of the very thing the establishment would most hate – disloyalty to Rome: *These men ... advocate customs that are not lawful for us as Romans to accept or practise.*

Just a few weeks later, a few miles down the road in Thessalonica, a similar thing happens:

> But the Jews were jealous, and taking some wicked men of the rabble, they formed a mob, set the city in uproar, and attacked the house of Jason, seeking to bring them out to the crowd. And when they could not find Paul, they dragged Jason and some of the brothers before the city authorities, shouting, 'these men who have turned the world upside

> down have come here also, and Jason has received them,
> and they are all acting against the decrees of Caesar, saying
> that there is another king, Jesus' (Acts 17:5-7).

So the hostility against Paul in Macedonia stems from greedy, pagan businessmen and from jealous Jews. Both groups saw their position threatened as Paul proclaimed Christ. Wanting to protect their position, their prestige, and their place in society, both the greedy businessmen and the jealous Jews accuse Paul to the authorities.

They choose the most public scenario possible – the market square! This is the equivalent to trial by media! Trial in the market square by mob rule. And they choose the key point of Paul's teaching that will threaten and upset the secular establishment: *They are advocating customs that are not lawful for us, as Romans, to accept* (16:21). *They are acting against the decrees of Caesar, saying there is another king, Jesus* (17:7).

The slave girl's owners and the Jews know precisely the point at which Paul's teaching will challenge the secular establishment: the gospel claim that Jesus Christ is Lord. And so they hand the Christians over to the Roman authorities to be imprisoned and beaten.

Now of course, there is nothing new here at all. This is precisely the kind of hostile opposition that Jesus faced: *So the chief priests and the Pharisees gathered the Council and said, 'What are we to do? For this man performs many signs. If we let him go on like this, everyone will believe in him, and the Romans will come and take away both our place and our nation'* (John 11:47). Here the opposition was spearheaded by the religious leaders wanting to protect their privileged position with the establishment.

Peter too faced the same kind of hostile opposition from the religious leaders: *but the high priest rose up, and all who were with him (that is, the party of the Sadducees), and filled with jealousy they arrested the apostles and put them in the public prison* (Acts 5:17).

Paul's own imprisonment in Rome came about because of the same kind of accusations made by Jews when he was in Jerusalem: *the Jews from Asia, seeing him (Paul) in the temple, stirred up the crowd and laid hands on him crying out, 'Men of Israel, help! This is the man who is teaching everyone everywhere against the people and the law and this place'* (Acts 21:27).

And now the Philippians were having similar experiences: *You are engaged in the **same** conflict that you saw **I had** and now hear that I **still have**.*

Indeed, this is what has happened every century down through the ages to the genuinely Christian Church in every age and every generation. Martin Luther and the sixteenth-century reformers, the Puritans in the seventeenth-century, and George Whitefield and John Wesley in the eighteenth-century, were all vigorously opposed by the unconverted religious leaders in the establishment as they proclaimed the gospel. The great social reforms brought in by Wilberforce and Shaftesbury were all opposed by greedy, secular parliamentarians who saw the Abolition of Slavery Act and the Factory Acts impacting on the profit margin of their businesses.

So there is nothing new about this hostile persecution that Paul is facing in his prison cell in Rome. There is nothing unique about the hostility that the model church in Philippi is facing. The question is: how does Paul, the model pastor, respond to this hostility from outside? The answer is there in verses 12-13: *what has happened to me has really served to advance the gospel so that it has become known throughout the whole imperial guard and to all the rest that my imprisonment is for Christ.*

It is a good thing, he says. There were approximately 9,000 soldiers in the Praetorian Guard in Rome. Some commentators question whether Paul is exaggerating here when he says that *the whole imperial guard* have come to know that his imprisonment is *for Christ*. But it is altogether possible that, as the guards changed and did their stint on duty, the news spread through all the different battalions of soldiers. After all, Paul was something of an unusual prisoner – he wasn't a common criminal. And as Paul continued proclaiming the gospel to each of his guards as they came on duty, so it became *known throughout the whole imperial guard and to all the rest (!) that my imprisonment is for* (literally *in*) *Christ.*

So the jealous Jews and the greedy businessmen have actually given Paul and, more importantly Jesus Christ, great publicity.

Not only so, but also the other Christian *brothers, having become confident in the Lord by my imprisonment, are much more bold to speak the Word without fear* (v. 14). All over Rome, the Christians were now beginning to speak openly and boldly about Jesus. This is what so often happens when persecution comes. The publicity sets people talking about Jesus and then Christians, emboldened by the suffering of some, speak out.

Now I hope we can see that Paul, by speaking so openly about himself to his partners in Philippi, will be a great encouragement to them and to all Christians around the world who suffer hostility. For God can take even the most vigorous hostility of those who are opposed to His gospel and use it to His advantage.

This is going to be an increasingly important lesson for us in the so-called 'Western world'. I am not the only one who anticipates a period of increased hostility towards the claim of the gospel that Jesus Christ is Lord, and that at His name *every knee will bow, in heaven and on earth and under the earth, and every tongue confess that Jesus Christ is Lord to the glory of God the Father* (2:10-11). Already we can see the Establishment church kowtowing to the multicultural demands of the state and watering down the message of the gospel into something more acceptable, a multi-faith mish-mash that denies the unique claims of Jesus.

Recent legislation in the UK Parliament has sought to make it more difficult to teach and live by the gospel. Both the Racial and Religious Hatred Bill in 2005 and the proposed regulations to prohibit discrimination on the grounds of sexual orientation under the Equality Act 2006, have sought to include aspects that would make open proclamation of the gospel more difficult. In her recent book, *Londonistan,* Melanie Phillips writes:

> Under the rubric of multiculturalism and promoting 'diversity', local authorities and government bodies are

systematically bullying Christianity out of existence. Christian voluntary groups fall foul of such bodies on the grounds that to be Christian suggests these groups are not committed to 'diversity'. So they are treated with suspicion even when they have a proven track record of success.[1]

Yet this hostility of state and religious establishment alike has given the gospel unexpected publicity. Even as I have been writing this book, the national newspapers have been reporting on an initiative run by Christians and introduced into Dartmoor prison by the prison chaplain. This work has been closed down by the prison authorities and by the local archdeacon – religious and secular authorities working in tandem – despite the fact that it has a proven track record in this country and abroad. It is understood by all to be successful in helping prisoners to reform, but it breaches the prison's 'diversity' policy both by proclaiming Jesus Christ as Lord and by promoting the unique virtue of heterosexual marriage. Hardly anyone would have heard of this great gospel ministry were it not for the hostility of the archdeacon and the prison authorities. Now the good work of gospel men and women has been published abroad to the whole nation through the broadsheets!

Paul says: *what has happened to me has really served to advance the gospel ... Christ is proclaimed, and in that I rejoice* (vv. 12, 18).

However, **hostility from the outside** is not the only thing that Paul and the Philippians are facing. Alongside the hostility from outside there is a **rivalry and jealousy from inside** as Paul and his gospel partners seek to spread

---

[1] Melanie Phillips, *Londonistan*, GSB p.116.

the gospel. So in verses 15–17 we are shown **the model pastor's response to rivalry from the inside.**

In the face of rivalry from within – praise God! The gospel is proclaimed

Paul again sees parallels between his own experience and that of the Philippian believers. He mentions the rivalry and envy that he is facing in Rome, because rivalry and jealousy are also being experienced within the church at Philippi as they engage in gospel work. In chapter 2:3, Paul tells them to *'do nothing from **rivalry or conceit.**'*, and offers his solution: *Let each of you look not only to his own interests but also to the interests of others'* (2:4) Here in chapter 1:15-18, however, Paul explains how he is able to rejoice in the face of envious rivalry even amongst the Christians in Rome.

Often verses 15-18 have been read as if some people in Rome are preaching a gospel that is slightly defective, but that Paul is glad, nonetheless, that at least something *near* the truth is being preached. But as we look at them closely, we can see that there are real problems with the view that these envious gospel preachers are doctrinally defective. Paul says that these rival preachers are *brothers* (the *some indeed* of verse 15 are the *brothers* of verse 14) who *speak the word without fear* and that they *preach Christ* (vv. 14-15). And in verses 17 and 18 he says that *Christ is proclaimed.* He couldn't possibly have said such things about a group of people who were preaching a defective gospel. So it isn't good enough just to say of these brothers that they were preaching broadly the kind of thing that Paul preached; or that they were a bit dodgy in some areas, but that otherwise they were OK! No! These Christians were doctrinally solid gospel brothers.

However, Paul says that as they preach the gospel, they do so out of *envy and rivalry*. Rivalry speaks of wanting to prevent a rival getting something. Envy speaks of wanting to gain that 'something' for yourself. Their preaching is a *pretence* (v. 18) – the word means 'a cover', 'a mask', and it is used of something that is done for personal selfish, motives. So Paul seems to be suggesting that in the Church in Rome, and in the Church in Philippi, the advance of the gospel message, with the hostility that it brings, can unearth real Christian brothers and sisters who are doing a clear Christian work, but from sinful motives.

Any of us who know anything of our own sinful human nature will be able to recognize this scenario immediately. We know from Paul's letter to Rome that the church there was going well. There were plenty of good, keen, strong and healthy Christians there. But with Paul's arrival in Rome, some of those who might previously have seen themselves as big hitters in the Roman scene could easily have had their noses put out of joint.

Just imagine the senior pastor of an imaginary St Helgar's Church at Emperor's Gate. He's used to calling the shots around Rome. But now Paul is here, and the senior pastor of St Helgar's feels a little threatened, a touch eclipsed. Then there is the leader of that smaller church in a run-down part of town, St Grudger's in Chip Street. Again, he has always been just a touch bitter and jealous that God has not given him a more high-profile ministry. He's always carping away at the bigger churches, and at the evangelists and church planters like Paul who travel the world doing gospel work. Once Paul gets put into jail, there is the perfect opportunity for any who are slightly envious of Paul to rub their hands together and to make personal profit from his trials. Perhaps they even suggested that Paul's suffering in jail was a result of his over-zealous activity, and that his imprisonment was an unnecessary setback for the gospel (v. 12).

Professor Don Carson puts it like this:

> Probably they magnify their own ministry by putting Paul down. We can imagine their own pompous reflections: 'it really is sad that so great a man as Paul has frittered away his gospel opportunities simply because he is so inflexible. After all, I and many others managed to remain at large and preach the gospel: one must assume that Paul has a deep character flaw that puts him in the path of trouble. **My** ministry is being blessed, while **he** languishes in prison.' Thus the more they speak, the more their own ways are justified, and the more Paul is made to look like a twit.[2]

It is not hard, is it, if we know anything about our own human nature, to see how envy, rivalry and pretence can creep into our motives for preaching the gospel – even in a model church like Philippi. It happens on youth camps in the summer. Someone else gives a really clear talk that is applauded by everybody. They **always** get asked to speak, but our own efforts at gospel service appear to go unrecognized. When eventually something goes wrong for them, how easy it is to cheer a little cheer. Someone else's

---

[2] D. A. Carson, *Basics for Believers*, IVP p.24.

house group or evangelistic work seems to flourish whilst yours plods along at rather a pedestrian pace. When a setback in their ministry is heard of, how easy it is secretly to feel pleased.

Just recently one of our most courageous, effective and energetic Christian leaders in England faced opposition from a bishop who has opposed many gospel initiatives. Eventually he had his licence to preach removed. It has been striking to me to have heard several other so-called 'evangelical' leaders, *brothers* even, using the opportunity of his hardship to snipe at his character. Some even wrote publicly against him: *some indeed preach Christ from envy and rivalry.*

Paul shows us in verse 18 how the **model pastor** should handle **rivalry from within :** *What then? Only that in every way, whether in pretence or in truth, Christ is proclaimed, and in that I rejoice.* God can use even the petty jealousies of small-minded ministers to bring about the proclamation of His gospel.

But if **hostility from without** and **rivalry from within** are currently causing Paul to rejoice at the preaching of the gospel in Rome, Paul goes on in verses 19-26 to speak about the future and his plans for the Philippians. It is clear that Paul is conscious that death is a likely outcome of his trial. But if he is to live, then there is only one thing on his mind: the proclamation of the gospel.

In any and every circumstance – praise God! The gospel is proclaimed

Verses 19-26 deal both with the possibility of Paul's death following his trial, and with his travel plans should he live.

Once again, Paul cannot help but 'look on the bright side of life'. Or should we say, the brighter side of death!

When Paul says his trial *will turn out for my deliverance* (v. 19), he is not talking about the outcome of the trial. The language being used here is lifted straight from the book of Job and from the Psalms, where the deliverance referred to is ultimate salvation by God. Similarly, when he speaks of *not being ashamed* in verse 20, the idea is of ultimate vindication by God. So Paul isn't referring to his immediate acquittal in verse 19. The outcome of the trial is still uncertain, which is why he speaks so openly about the possibility of his death. What is certain to Paul is that Christ will *be honoured in my body whether by life or by death.* And he is sure that Christ will be honoured, because he is preparing to defend and confirm the gospel at his trial. The word translated *with full courage* could equally be read 'with full outspokenness'. Even in his trial, with his life on the line, Paul is going to make sure that the gospel is proclaimed. Notice, though, that this isn't Paul doing it on his own. If it weren't for verse 19 we might think that Paul was entirely self-sufficient. That would be a huge mistake. Rather it is only *through your prayers and the help of the Spirit of Jesus Christ* that Paul is expecting to speak out openly in front of the Roman Emperor and thus honour Christ and find vindication on the Day of Christ.

So once again, quite extraordinarily, Paul sees his trial – where death is a most likely outcome – to be an opportunity for the proclamation of the gospel. And what if he is not sentenced to death? Well then, he will continue to serve the Philippians selflessly.

Verses 21-26 demonstrate that Paul has what I like to call a single-minded double-mindedness or a single-minded schizophrenia. His great concern, above everything else, is to be in heaven with Jesus. But as he looks for that day, which is entirely in the hands of Jesus, he has his eye on his gospel partners in Philippi. Such is his Christ-like, selfless love for them, that he is compelled to make plans for them even as he faces his own possible demise.

The words *hard pressed* contain a graphic image which speaks of an equal force being exerted on both sides, so that Paul is constrained and driven forward. As Paul looks to heaven, and as he looks to his partners in Philippi, he experiences an equal compulsion from two opposite directions. On the one hand he sees the glorious prospect of death and going to be with the Lord – *that is better by far.* On the other hand, he sees the opportunity for yet more gospel proclamation – *if I am to live in the flesh that means fruitful labour for me.* But Paul is convinced of the need of the Philippians and so, selflessly and sacrificially, he makes plans to visit them: *convinced of this I know that I will remain and continue with you all for your progress and joy in the faith.*

Paul is deliberately tailoring his personal testimony to encourage the Philippians. They have been facing **hostility** from without, they have been experiencing **rivalry** within, and they too have been aware of **affliction** and the temptation to give up. By sharing his testimony as he anticipates his trial, Paul gives the model response to each of these situations. He is able to 'look on the bright side', for at every point he is seeking first to proclaim Christ.

As he makes the most of every opportunity, this priority transforms his perspective and his experience.

I wonder what it is that gives you joy such that you delight and rejoice with thankfulness in every situation? I remember watching the highlights of the European Championship Cup Final 2006. At the close of play the cameras panned around the ground catching the reactions of players and crowds alike. On one side of the pitch there were scenes of utter desolation and dejected disappoint-ment. One small girl was caught on screen with her face painted in the colours of her team – tears streaming down her painted cheeks. On the other side there was joy and delight, rejoicing and celebration. Fans and players were united in overwhelming euphoria at what had happened that night.

For Paul it is the proclamation of the gospel that causes his heart to fill with joyful thanksgiving. For this reason he is able to rejoice in any and every circumstance. When he is facing hostility, he rejoices – for this gives him further opportunity to proclaim Christ. When he faces rivalry, he rejoices – for the rivalry results in further proclamation of Jesus. When he faces death, he rejoices – and makes plans for yet more gospel proclamation, for to die and be with the Lord *is gain.*

Questions:

1. The passage breaks down in three sections: verses 12-14, verses 15-18, verses 19-26. What is the particular difficulty Paul faces in each of these sections?

2. The Christians who proclaim Christ in verses 15-18 are real and genuine Christian brothers proclaiming a doctrinally pure gospel. What is wrong with their motives?

3. How is it that in spite of all the difficulties mentioned in the three sections, Paul is still able to *rejoice* (v. 18)?

4. What does this tell us about Paul's priorities?

5. Paul's *deliverance* in verse 19 and his being *not at all ashamed* refer to his final salvation and God's vindication of him. What part do his Philippian partners play in this?

6. How have your own priorities and plans been challenged by what Paul has shared of his testimony? What causes you to rejoice?

THREE

Citizens of Heaven Contending for the Faith of the Gospel

Philippians 1:27–2:4

²⁷ Only let your manner of life be worthy of the gospel of Christ, so that whether I come and see you or am absent, I may hear of you that you are standing firm in one spirit, with one mind striving side by side for the faith of the gospel, ²⁸ and not frightened in anything by your opponents. This is a clear sign to them of their destruction, but of your salvation, and that from God. ²⁹ For it has been granted to you that for the sake of Christ you should not only believe in him but also suffer for his sake, ³⁰ engaged in the same conflict that you saw I had and now hear that I still have.

^{2:1} So if there is any encouragement in Christ, any comfort from love, any participation in the Spirit, any affection and sympathy, ² complete my joy by being of the same mind, having the same love, being in full accord and of one mind. ³ Do nothing from rivalry or conceit, but in humility count others more significant than yourselves. ⁴ Let each of you look not only to his own interests, but also to the interests of others.

Philippians chapter 1:27 through to chapter 4:1 form the heart of Paul's letter.[1] Paul has brought his gospel partners in Philippi up to date with his own situation and he has expressed his prayerful praise for their partnership. Now he turns to speak to them directly. As he addresses them, Paul's aim is to strengthen their partnership. He does this by using the language of citizenship.

At a time when migration, asylum and identity cards are so very much in the UK news, this concept of citizenship is rather topical. However, we need to be clear that Paul's concern is not with earthly, national citizenship. He isn't going to be talking about being Australian, Spanish, Iraqi, American or even British. No! Paul's concern is with heavenly citizenship and membership of God's kingdom. His purpose is to develop and strengthen the Philippians in effective partnership as like-minded, clear-thinking citizens of heaven, committed to the advance of the public truth that Jesus Christ is Lord.

We can see that **citizenship** is the issue that binds this section together by looking at 1:27 and 3:20. Paul introduces this section by turning to the Philippians and urging them to *stand firm* as citizens behaving in a manner worthy of the gospel. Chapter 1:27-28 is probably the key to the whole of this letter. It begins: *Only let your manner of life be worthy of the gospel of Christ so that whether I come and see you or am absent I may hear that you are standing firm.* The phrase *manner of life* translates a Greek word meaning 'to have one's citizenship'. The ESV footnote translates it: *only behave as citizens worthy*. So the issue here is citizenship.

---

[1] See Gordon Fee, *Paul's letter to the Philippians*, NICNT, Eerdmans p.158ff

At the other end of this section, having explained what it means to *stand firm as citizens,* Paul restates his point. Christians are *citizens of heaven,* waiting eagerly for their Saviour from there, so they are to *stand firm.* He concludes: *But our citizenship is in heaven and from it we await a Saviour, the Lord Jesus Christ ... therefore my brothers ... stand firm thus in the Lord, my beloved* (3:20; 4:1).

Let me make three general observations about this citizenship. First, when Paul tells the Philippians to *behave as citizens worthy of the gospel of Christ* (v. 27), he is making the **assumption** that they are already citizens of heaven. In chapter 3:20 he declares: *But our citizenship is in heaven.* Note the use of the present tense! As a result of Jesus' death on the cross, the Philippian believers have been made blameless and pure, and have been declared to be right with God (1:11). Paul can say with absolute confidence and assurance that they already belong to the kingdom of the One who has been declared Lord and King, before whom *every knee in heaven and on earth and under the earth will bow* (2:10).

This is important for us. The Christian who trusts in Jesus has already been given membership of God's kingdom. I frequently come across people who call themselves 'Christians', but who see themselves rather like an asylum seeker desperately trying to meet the criteria for citizenship in a host country. But the Christian is a *citizen* already! It is a present reality. We do not have to earn brownie points in order to gain access to God's Kingdom or collect air miles to make it to heaven. The work of Jesus on our behalf guarantees our citizenship.

I wish I could ask you to take out your passport at this point. Mine happens to be British. It contains a photograph of me that looks as if it might have been taken when I was serving time in one of Her Majesty's corrective institutions! It states that Taylor, William Thomas, born ... (a date which we do not need to dwell on at this point!), is a British citizen. It is incontrovertible proof of my membership. It is a guarantee. I belong – and I have the absolute right to all the benefits and privileges of being a British citizen. For the Christian, membership of heaven is guaranteed as we trust in Him, by the work of Jesus on the cross on our behalf, by His victory over death and by His exaltation to reign as King. All the benefits and privileges of heavenly citizenship are ours. So, says Paul, *stand firm! Only behave as citizens worthy* (1:27); *our citizenship is in heaven ... stand firm thus in the Lord, my beloved* (3:20–4:1).

Secondly, not only is citizenship **assumed**, citizenship is also **understood.** When Paul uses the language of *citizenship* the Philippians know precisely what he is talking about.

Acts 16:12 says that Philippi was *a leading city of the district of Macedonia and a Roman colony*. The city of Philippi had been granted Roman citizenship back in 31 BC, after Octavian had defeated Antony and Cleopatra. The whole city of Philippi came under Roman governance, which meant that there was legal protection for the Roman citizens under the Roman legal system. The benefits of being a Roman colony in the Roman Empire, at a time when Rome ruled the whole of the known world, were immense. Roman citizens could travel freely. Businesses enjoyed immediate global reach and global trust. Roman citizenship was a passport to progress, privilege and status. It is not hard, then, to imagine the civic pride of the Philippians. They had a special relationship with the sole global superpower and they stood shoulder to shoulder with the Roman Emperor.

So the concept of citizenship is understood by Paul's audience. But, says Paul, now you need to remember that you Christians are first and foremost *citizens of heaven.* You await a Saviour from there. All the benefits, privileges and status of the new heaven and new earth are yours. So are the responsibilities to *behave as worthy citizens of heaven.* So *stand firm!*

Citizenship is **assumed**. Citizenship is **understood**. Thirdly, citizenship is **corporate.**

Standing firm as a citizen of heaven is not something that we do on our own. There is nothing Christian about being a lone-ranger disciple. Again, Paul makes the point in verse 27: *Only behave as citizens worthy of the gospel of Christ, so that ... I may hear that you are standing firm in* **one spirit, with one mind.** Paul's point here is that we are united as citizens of heaven by the one Holy Spirit. It is He who has brought us into this heavenly Kingdom. As citizens of heaven, then, we are to share *one mind.* In fact the word Paul uses here means 'single-souled'. The soul refers to what we truly are. The same idea is restated in 2:2: *complete my joy by being of the same* **mind,** *having the same love, being in full accord* ('single-souled') *and of* **one mind.**

The point is that we are to share **one mind.** This is such a big idea in Philippians that it is worth pausing for a moment. The **mind** does not refer merely to our intellect.

One commentator puts it like this: 'the mind, or soul, ... points to what we feel about things and how we react to them. It raises the question of what things we consider valuable and what constitutes a worthwhile objective in life.' Sometimes over breakfast, we look together with our children at the passage we are going to be studying as a church family in the Sunday sermon. Just recently I was talking with my children about these verses, and we came to the bit about *the mind* and began to explore what it meant. One of the children chipped in: 'So, Daddy, you mean that it's **what we are on the inside.**' Precisely! Now, says Paul, *stand firm* behaving as *citizens worthy of the gospel in one Spirit, with one 'what-you-are-on-the-inside'*.

Once we see it like that, it isn't at all hard to work out what Paul is saying. We are all used to the idea of citizens sharing the same loves, the same concerns and the same ideas as to what is important, the idea of a shared national mindset – a shared sense of what is valuable and of first priority, and of what is a major concern. For instance, what is it people say about the Japanese? That they have a great sense of honour and of dignity. What is said about the French? That they are charming, intelligent, exquisitely sophisticated in their culinary skills.

What of the English? Perhaps we would rather not know! I once sat at a table of French friends after one of our church meetings and asked them what they say about the English: 'We would rather not talk about that over lunch,' they replied! When Paul says *only behave as citizens worthy of the gospel ... standing firm, in one Spirit, with one mind*, his concern is that we do not stand firm with the prevailing citizenry values of Rome, but with the shared, single-souled citizenry values of heaven. The same '**what we are on the inside**'.

If we trust Jesus and belong to Him, then our citizenship of heaven is guaranteed. We all understand what citizen-ship means, but now, as Christians, we have a new first loyalty and a new citizenry home. We are to share the values, priorities and concerns of Jesus' kingdom first and foremost. They are to come over and above the values and mindset of whatever nation, social set, club or family we come from.

But that leaves us asking the question, what is it that *standing firm* as citizens worthy of heaven actually looks like? And that takes us to the first of our three major points. For the command to *stand firm* is the main verb in verse 27, but the main verb *stand firm* is then qualified by further participles (action words) that explain what it looks like to *stand firm* as worthy citizens.

Contending corporately for the public truth of the Christian message

The reason I say that we are to contend for the public truth of the Christian message is because Paul speaks in verse 27 of *striving side by side* for *the faith of the gospel*. Paul isn't speaking here about something vague and subjective. He is speaking about the objective truth that Jesus Christ has been appointed by God as the universal king and ruler who has been *highly exalted* and has *bestowed on him the name that is above every name so that at the name of Jesus every knee should bow, in heaven and on earth and under the earth, and every tongue confess that Jesus Christ is Lord* (2:9-11).

This is the first mark, then, of a true citizen of heaven who is standing firm and behaving in a manner worthy. It is that we *strive side by side* for this public truth.

The word *striving* is frequently translated *contending*. It is a term which comes from the athletics track, the Olympic arena. In fact we get our word *athletics* from the word that Paul uses here. The picture is of an energetic, athletic pursuit of a single goal – the public proclamation of the truth that Jesus Christ is Lord. But Paul does a quite brilliant thing with this word *striving*. Instead of simply using the verb ' to strive', he forms a new word by sticking the phrase 'together with' on the front of it. That's why our translation has *striving **side by side***. It could equally be 'togetherstriving'! So we are not thinking here about an individual event. This is partnership again. An energetic, athletic pursuit as a whole team.

There was a quite beautiful illustration of this in the 3,000m steeplechase race at the 2004 Olympics in Athens. The Kenyans have won gold in this race at every games since they started competing in 1968. It is a monopoly they are not keen to relinquish! However in 2004, as they entered the final lap the Kenyans were coming first, second and fourth. The great athlete Ezekiel Kemboi was leading, but as he looked back he saw that there was a possibility of their sweeping the medals board. So, instead of racing on to the tape, he slowed right down and started to urge and cajole his fellow Kenyans. To the horror of the BBC commentator, Brendan Foster, he turned the individual event into a team sport. He went alongside his team-mates Brimin Kipruto and Paul Kipsiele Koech and urged them on. Then, when they crossed the line in gold, silver and bronze positions, they ran their victory lap together, clad in one Kenyan national flag as they danced and hugged their way around the track. This is the kind of teamwork that Paul has in mind as he speaks of 'togetherstriving' for *the faith of the gospel* – though the hugging and dancing is optional!

Paul's expectation for Christian businessmen or women in Philippi was that, as they got up at 5.30 a.m. to start the day, their priorities would be crystal clear: 'I am a citizen of **heaven** first and foremost. Today, as I stand firm, my business, above all else, is to contend side by side with others for the public truth of the gospel.'

Paul's expectation for the Christian teacher, student, nurse or parent in Philippi was that as they entered the staff room, lecture hall, hospital or playground, they too would be crystal clear about their priorities: 'I am a citizen of **heaven** first and foremost. Today my chief concern as I stand firm will be to strive side by side with others for the public truth of the gospel.'

The same priority should shape the behaviour of every Christian in every age, whether shopworker, lawyer, carer, doctor, soldier, pilot, or whatever. We are not to strive with the loneliness of the long-distance runner, or the isolation of the special forces operative hidden deep behind enemy lines. We are not to lock ourselves in our offices or behind our front doors. Rather we are to seek out other Christians and join with others in order to 'togetherstrive' for *the faith of the gospel.* That may mean setting up a Christian meeting in our school, factory or regiment. It may mean finding some way, with others, to introduce people to the truth of Jesus in our hospital or office. It will certainly mean being a part of a church where *striving side by side for the faith of the gospel* is the number-one priority.

But contending or striving isn't the only concept that spells out what it means to *stand firm* as we *behave in a manner worthy of the gospel.*

Contending courageously for the public truth of the Christian message

Verses 28-30 indicate that the Philippians were experiencing hostility and opposition of the same kind that Paul was facing in Rome as he wrote, and that Paul had faced when he was with them in Philippi: *For it has been granted to you that for the sake of Christ you should not only believe in Him but also suffer for His sake, engaged in the same conflict that you **saw** I had and now hear that I **still** have.*

The nature of that opposition is described in Acts 16:16-24. We have already seen that this opposition came from greedy, pagan businessmen who feared that Paul's public preaching of the gospel was going to cause a reduction in their profits. You will remember that they handed Paul over to the magistrates in the market square and accused him of *advocating customs that are not lawful for us as Roman citizens to accept or practise* (Acts 16:21). To the townspeople of Philippi, with their civic pride and valued possession of Roman citizenship, this was a serious accusation. A similar charge was levelled at Jason just a few miles down the road in Thessalonica: *they are acting against the decrees of Caesar, saying that there is another king, Jesus* (Acts 17:7).

So the charge was one of uncitizenry behaviour. It was brought by business people who feared that the changes the gospel brings to people's lives would affect their profits. It was brought by jealous Jews who feared that the challenge the gospel brings would affect their influence and privileges. As Paul taught the gospel there in Philippi, what he said was seen to be a threat to the status quo.

Inevitably, the gospel will have that effect. Once people realise that there is another King – Jesus – then their primary allegiance will change. Their first loyalty will be to their Heavenly King. In spite of the fact that Jesus teaches us that we should obey the earthly authorities, people who feel threatened by our new primary allegiance will oppose us. They will accuse us of rocking the boat, of being awkward, unnecessarily provocative or inflexible.

Imagine how this might have impacted on Lydia, the first Philippian convert. We read about her in Acts 16:11-15. She was a dealer in purple cloth from the city of Thyatira, but she had set up her business in Philippi, which is where Paul met her as he preached the gospel by the riverside. She was obviously a successful businesswoman in the city. Having moved to the leading city of Philippi, with all its connections to the major markets of Rome, she was probably looking to expand her business. Perhaps purple was 'in' that season!

But Lydia had become a Christian. She had recognized the truth that Jesus has been declared Lord and King of heaven and earth. Now, in her business practice, she was going to *stand firm, striving for the faith of the gospel.* At the annual dinner in the Cloth Workers' Guild it would no doubt have been the custom to toast the Emperor. The Emperor in Roman times was understood to be in some sense divine. Now, as the other business people rose to lift their goblets and drink the toast, what was Lydia to do? As she stood firm she would certainly stand out. She was clearly going to rock the status quo. She would have to be inflexible at this point as she insisted that *'there is another King – Jesus'!* And this would result in hostility and opposition – Lydia didn't quite fit in any more.

Or imagine that Lydia had a potential new client coming across from Rome to talk about a trade deal. There was a possibility of new markets and lucrative new outlets. But this client was used to being entertained in ways in which a Christian would find it impossible to participate. Now that Lydia had become a Christian, she recognized that Jesus has been declared Lord and King of heaven and earth. As she spent time with this new client, she was going to *stand firm, striving for the faith of the gospel.* She was certainly going to stand out. She would be different. She wouldn't be 'playing the game' at this point, and probably this would result in hostility and opposition – she didn't quite fit in any more. She might even lose out on potentially lucrative new business.

Then, over time, there were other workers from Philippi who called themselves Christians. They met one lunchtime during the week, and they even met before work on occasion to pray together. They wouldn't keep quiet about this new message about *another King – Jesus,* and it was suspected that they *advocate customs that are not lawful for us as Romans to accept.* Lydia would have to make the decision as to whether she was going to join with them. Many of them weren't of her status or seniority in the city. Surely she didn't meet with them, did she? As she began to contend side by side for the truth of the gospel, she would certainly stand out.

It's not hard to see how the pressure might increase as awareness of the good news of the Christian gospel grew in Philippi. Inevitably, when we become citizens of heaven, our allegiances change. This has an impact on every area of life as we *strive side by side for the faith of the gospel.* The new allegiance of the Christian to Christ alone soon begins to challenge the status quo of our social set, of our non-Christian family, of other members of the golf club or the office.

One young graduate worker at a big bank in the City recently spoke openly about her Christian views on human sexuality with another worker over coffee. The next day she was called to the human resources department. She was asked to leave.

A senior surgeon was open and public about the gospel, sharing his faith unashamedly as he contended with others for the truth of the gospel. He was removed from his position.

A young Thai student joined with 10,000 other students for her matriculation ceremony in the City Square of her university. Part of the ceremony involved each faculty group standing, turning to the statue of the Emperor after whom the university was named and bowing in worship.

The student had recently become a Christian. As the other 500 in her year group bowed, she alone remained standing. That year she was the only student in her faculty who was not issued with the highly prized faculty jacket.

I teach the Bible in the business district of London known as the City. Just a quarter of a mile up the road from the City there is a whole string of lap-dancing clubs. In addition, the police tell me, there are up to ten brothels operating within the City. It is not hard to imagine what would happen to those 'businesses' if the Christian gospel began to impact on the City once again, not to mention the effect on the new Government-backed casinos or on much of the advertising industry.

In the so-called 'Western world' over the last one hundred years, Christians have been able to *strive side by side for the faith of the gospel* with relative freedom. However, this is all in the process of changing. In many Western cultures there has been a determined effort to enshrine human rights legislation within the legal framework of our nations. Much of this human rights legislation provides good and valuable protection for people who might otherwise suffer discrimination. However, in a significant number of places, this new legislation clashes with *the faith of the gospel.* This is most obviously seen in the unique and exclusive claims of the Christian faith about Jesus, and in the Bible's teaching about sexuality. It will not be long before one or another minority pressure group begins to accuse Christians of *customs that are not lawful for us as* British *citizens to accept.* For we have *another King – Jesus,* and our citizenship demands that we contend publicly for *the faith of the gospel*.

The *citizen of heaven* who *stands firm, striving side by side for the faith of the gospel*, will face opposition. The mark of our *standing* will be that we remain unmoved and keep on speaking out just as Paul did in his trial and imprisonment in Rome. As we do so, this will be a clear sign to our opponents *of their destruction, but of our salvation* (v. 28), for as we stand with and for Jesus, here will be evidence that we belong to the One who has been declared by God to be *above every other name* and before whom *every knee will bow* (2:9, 10). We will be demonstrating that our *citizenship is in heaven* from where *we await a Saviour* (3:20). Meanwhile, those who oppose us will be showing, by their hostility, that they do not stand with the Lord and King of God's Kingdom. Indeed, they are against Him. This is a sure sign of their ultimate destruction.

So the citizen of heaven who stands will be one who contends **corporately** for *the faith of the gospel* and one who contends **courageously** for *the faith of the gospel*. But Paul has a third expectation of the heavenly citizen.

Contending selflessly for the public truth of the Christian message

In the first four verses of chapter 2, Paul expands on the **shared genetic code** of the citizens of heaven, then he outlines the **corporate concerns** of the citizens of heaven, and finally he spells out the **particular personal priority** of the citizens of heaven.

The **shared genetic** code is there in verse 1 of chapter 2: *So, if there is any encouragement in Christ, any comfort from love, any participation in the Spirit, any affection and sympathy....*

We can see straightaway three supernatural realities that have come into the lives of all true believers. The energizing *encouragement* of Christ, the comforting *love* of God and the *participation* (it's that word 'partnership' again) in the Spirit, which lead to a mutual affection and concern for one another. This is our shared genetic inheritance as citizens of heaven.

There were places thirty or forty years ago, in some of the more remote areas of England, where you could almost tell which village a person came from. People didn't move around so much in those days, so the same families might have lived in the same parts of rural England for many years. You could go to certain parts of the country and find a striking similarity in looks, in behaviour, in mannerisms and in attitudes. There was a shared genetic inheritance.

Paul's point is that we citizens of heaven are all united through the same shared Spiritual genes. Have you at any time, in any way, had any personal experience of the grace of the Lord Jesus, the love of God and the fellowship of the Holy Spirit? Of course you have! If you haven't, then you can't possibly call yourself a Christian. These are the very hallmarks of what makes a Christian. This is our shared genetic inheritance.

All of this is framed in terms of an appeal. In the original Greek each of the clauses begins with *if. If there is any encouragement ... if there is any comfort ... if there is any participation.* It's as if Paul is saying to these Christians in

Philippi: as Christians *surely* you have been encouraged as you stand firm in the face of opposition by the grace of Jesus that guarantees your place in heaven. As Christians, *surely* you have been comforted as you strive side by side in the face of opposition by the *love* of God that assures you that He loves you enough to send His only Son to die for you. As Christians, *surely* you have experienced personally the presence of the Spirit who energizes and enables you in the Christian life and fills you with affection and concern for one another.

So then, given that God has been at work in all of us in this way, we should have **corporate common concerns:** ... *complete my joy by being of the same mind, having the same love, being in full accord and of one mind* (v. 2).

The point is not that we should all look the same – or even act exactly the same way in every situation. Paul is not arguing here for a monochrome homogeneity amongst Christians. He doesn't expect us all to have the same tastes, wear the same clothes or listen to the same music – what a relief! We are not cult members! But we are to have the same mindset, the same 'what we are on the inside'.

We shall see just what this *mind* of the heavenly citizen should look like in the next chapter of the book as we look at the mind of Christ. For now, notice how Paul insists that his partners in the gospel should share the same mind. He says it in four different ways, repeating himself twice over. We are to have *the same mind* and we are to be of *one mind*. We are to have *the same love* and we are to be *in full accord* (literally 'single-souled'). All of this comes from the One Lord Jesus, the One Heavenly Father and the One Holy Spirit at work within us.

This **corporate common concern** should result in a **particular personal priority** for the heavenly citizen: the priority of selfless love and sacrificial concern for others. Paul writes: *Do nothing from rivalry or conceit, but in humility count others more significant than yourselves. Let each of you look not only to his own interests, but also to the interests of others* (vv. 3-4). This is how we are to stand firm as citizens of heaven, behaving in a manner that is worthy of our citizenship.

Each of us now holds dual citizenship. Yes, we are citizens of England, Wales or Scotland, Australia or France, for instance. The New Testament teaches us to recognize earthly authorities, and we are to take our place as citizens in the culture of which we are a part. But the Christian person now has a higher allegiance and a higher priority. Our primary calling is to live as citizens of heaven and to behave in a manner that is governed by heaven's values and heaven's concerns.

Standing firm as citizens of heaven means contending **corporately (side by side)** for the public truth that Jesus is Lord – *the faith of the gospel*. This is now our priority wherever we find ourselves.

Standing firm as citizens of heaven means contending **courageously** in the face of opposition. The very fact of our citizenship means that we will rock the status quo and therefore face opposition. As we stand firm we shall confirm our own citizenship and our opponents will confirm their citizenship too.

Standing firm as citizens of heaven means contending **selflessly** for the public truth of the gospel.

Our behaviour will now be shaped by the mindset of heaven. And, as we are going to see in the next chapter, the mindset of heaven is that of a selfless, sacrificial concern for the sake of others. Our shared heavenly genetic code will show itself in a shared common concern. Our shared common concern will result in a particular personal priority that puts the eternal well-being and interest of others in front of our own. We will value other people. We will see their needs as more significant than ours. We will battle against the temptation to rivalry and personal ego trips.

Questions:

1. These verses describe what it is like to stand firm with our manner of life worthy of the gospel of Christ. What does Paul expect us to do as we stand firm?

2. In what different ways does this passage expand on the nature of partnership in the gospel?

3. How is it that our standing firm in the face of opposition acts as a sign?

4. In what ways are you currently striving side by side with others for the public truth of the gospel?

5. Where do you think Christians are facing opposition today?

6. In what ways are you tempted to act out of rivalry, conceit or self-interest? What is the antidote (from the passage)?

FOUR

The Heavenly Mindset

Philippians 2:5-11(NIV)

⁵ Your attitude should be the same as that of Christ Jesus:
⁶ Who, being in very nature God, did not consider equality
with God something to be grasped, ⁷ but made himself
nothing, taking the very nature of a servant, being made
in human likeness. And being found in appearance as a
man, ⁸ he humbled himself and became obedient to death
– even death on a cross! ⁹ Therefore God exalted him to the
highest place and gave him the name that is above every
name, ¹⁰ that at the name of Jesus every knee should bow,
in heaven and on earth and under the earth, ¹¹ and every
tongue confess that Jesus Christ is Lord, to the glory of God
the Father.

The aim of these verses is to reshape our minds. It is as if
Paul wants to get the spiritual equivalent of a surgical saw,
or a hammer and chisel, to lift the lid of our cranial plate,
to peer inside and examine our mindset in order to see if it
really is the mindset of a heavenly citizen.

We have already seen that all of us who trust in Jesus Christ are citizens of heaven. As Christian men or women, we can confidently call ourselves citizens of heaven, for that is where our true citizenship lies. It is secure already. Christian men or women, as citizens of heaven, are to stand firm together and contend for the public truth of the gospel of Jesus Christ. We are partners committed to the public proclamation of God's truth for the world.

Paul has urged us, therefore, as heavenly citizens to have a shared heavenly mindset. In chapter 2:2, he appealed to the Philippians: *complete my joy by being of the same mind, having the same love, being* (literally) *single-souled, and of one mind.*

It is as if Paul is saying: Look! If you are a genuine citizen of heaven then you should share with all other citizens of heaven an attitude or a mindset of purposeful, sacrificial, selfless service for the sake of the eternal well-being of others.

We have already seen that the *mind* in the Bible refers to 'what we feel about things and how we react to them. It raises the question of what things we consider valuable and what constitutes a worthwhile objective in life.'[1] You will remember that we described this as: 'what we are on the inside'.

In these verses Paul wants to get to work on our minds – the way we see things, our attitudes, values and ambitions, the aims and goals that govern the way we end up acting. He does this by directing our attention to the chief citizen

---

[1] J. A. Motyer, *The Message of Philippians*, BST, IVP p. 95.

of heaven – the Lord Jesus Christ. All of this is clear from verse 5: *Have this mind among yourselves, which is yours in Christ Jesus ....*

So what is the mindset of the Chief Citizen, Jesus Christ?

The mindset of heaven is a mindset of selfless service

The point of verses 6-7 is not that Jesus exchanged the form of God for the form of a slave, so that when He became a slave He was in some sense not really showing us God. Rather that, as God, Jesus became a slave. This means that as we see God in Jesus, we see that God is prepared to take every advantage, every privilege and every possession and to use all that He has as an opportunity for unreserved self-sacrifice on behalf of His people. In order for us to see that this is the point Paul is making, we need to look at three technical words in verses 6 and 7.

The first is the word translated as *grasped at*. You can imagine that those who have wanted to deny that Jesus was God have used this word to argue that Jesus renounced all his divinity and became merely human. A man called R. W. Hoover has done a huge amount of research on the use of the word 'to grasp at' in the Greek language. He has shown conclusively that 'in every instance which I have examined this idiomatic expression refers to something already present and at one's disposal ... so the question is not whether one possesses something, but whether one chooses to exploit something.'[2] So Paul's point here is not

---

[2] Quoted in Peter O'Brien, *Commentary on Philippians*, NIGTC, Eerdmans p.215.

that Jesus wasn't God and chose not, as one who wasn't God, to grasp after equality with God. Rather Paul's point is that Jesus was God and yet He did not consider His position something to be exploited for his own advantage.

The word translated as *'made himself nothing'* is literally 'emptied Himself'. Some late nineteenth/twentieth-century writers have suggested that, in becoming man, Jesus became little more than a first-century prophet. But, as Alec Motyer puts it: 'it is not *of what* did Jesus empty himself? But *into what* did he empty himself? Paul is concerned not with what Jesus emptied himself *out of* but with what Jesus emptied himself *into.*'[3] *He made himself* – His whole self – *nothing, taking the form of a servant.* Again, F. F. Bruce puts it well: it is not 'that He exchanged the form of God for the form of a slave, but that He manifested the form of God in the form of a slave'. Divine equality meant sacrificial self-giving.[4]

The word *servant* is literally 'slave' – one with no rights, no rank, no privilege, no power, no significance and no status other than as one who is there to serve.

All this may seem a bit technical, but the point is that Jesus used the wealth, power, privilege and prestige of his position not for self-advancement, but to take on the form of a slave in order to serve His people.

The really big discovery for me, however, as I started to study this passage, is there in the second word of verse 6. The phrase translated in the ESV as *'though He was in the form of God'*, is more accurately translated by the NIV as

---

[3] J A Motyer, *The Message of Philippians*, BST, IVP p.113.

[4] See Peter O'Brien, *Commentary on Philippians*, NIGTC, Eerdmans p. 216.

'being in very nature God', which carries the sense of *'since Jesus was in the form of God'*, or *'precisely because Jesus was in the form of God'*[5]. In other words, Jesus acted the way He did because He **was** God.

Jesus didn't use all that He had for his own self-advancement. He didn't cling to His status.

He didn't hang on to his reputation. Instead He emptied Himself, His whole self, as God, into the form of a slave to serve selflessly, precisely because this is the very nature of God.

There is a place in Scotland where I love to fish. It's a pool called The Bulwark. At that point all the water of the river, every millilitre, passes for a brief moment through a tiny gorge. It's as if all the energy, life and power of the water, gathered over hundreds of square kilometres of the Cairngorms, is concentrated in that one, small channel. For me, that illustrates what Paul is saying in verse 7: God, in all his fullness, chose to concentrate all the energy, force, life and power of His being into the human form of Jesus Christ.

Of course, the fact that all God's power was concentrated in the baby Jesus explains why, as He grew up, His actions demonstrated this. Eyewitnesses of His life tell us that He spent his life doing extraordinary, God-like things. He turned water into wine. He healed a child on his deathbed. He emptied the hospitals of Galilee. He caused a paralysed, withered man to rise up after thirty-eight years on his mattress. He fed five thousand people. He walked

---

[5] See Peter O'Brien, *Commentary on Philippians*, NIGTC, Eerdmans pp. 215-16.

on water. But Paul tells us that the most God-like thing He did was to choose not to exploit His own divine power for personal gain. Instead, He chose to empty Himself into the form of a slave.

Each year in the City of London there is a ceremony in the Guildhall for the changing over of the Lord Mayor of London. It is called the Silent Ceremony and dates from at least the seventeenth century. Sweet-smelling herbs are scattered on the floor. Grown men walk around carrying bunches of flowers. The cast look to all intents as if they've just walked out of the set of *The Mikado*. (For the uninitiated, that's a satirical operetta set in Imperial Japan!) I was once in attendance at the ceremony as a chaplain. At the heart of the ceremony is the stripping from the old Lord Mayor of all the badges of office. The mace (symbol of his authority) is removed. His cloak is stripped off. The Lord Mayor's chain of office is taken from him. He arrives in pomp and splendour, but leaves a mere pauper. (Well, actually he left in a Daimler, but for the sake of the illustration we need to forget that bit!)

I remember thinking at the time that it was in some way a great illustration of the selfless sacrifice of Christ. However, as I've studied this passage, and as I've thought about what Paul is telling us, I've realized that it is absolutely not what we have here. For the Lord Mayor is stripped of his robes of office and is no longer Lord Mayor as he leaves the Guildhall. Paul's point is that **because** Jesus was God, **as** God and **while** He was God, Jesus emptied all of His divinity into the form of a slave.

It would illustrate the point much more closely if we were to head down into the basement of the Guildhall only to find the Lord Mayor himself, in all his splendour and glory, dressed in his mayoral robes, cleaning the urinals with a loo brush in one hand and a bottle of Harpic in the other.

The point of this glorious description of Jesus in chapter 2 is that at the heart of heaven is a mindset of selfless service for the sake of others:

> As God, Jesus stepped from His throne of glory in heaven.
> As God, Jesus entered the stable.
> As God, Jesus took up the towel and the basin and washed His disciples' feet.
> As God, Jesus prayed in the Garden.
> As God, Jesus was arrested.
> As God, He was beaten.
> As God, He was nailed to a cross.

All this so that now, seated on the throne of heaven, there is one who has shown us that the very essence of His nature is selfless service for the sake of His people.

I wonder if that changes our view of God at all? Or of heaven? Sometimes we can think of God as if He were some sort of bully, a demanding, self-serving despot, a taskmaster who is little more than a celestial traffic-enforcement officer wanting to squeeze tribute out of us by extortion. Here we are being shown that the true nature of God is selfless service for the sake of His people.

Paul's aim is that this attitude or *mind*, which is ours already in Christ Jesus, should become more and more a reality in the way we conduct ourselves. We belong to the chief model citizen – the Lord Jesus Christ. His very being is one of selfless, humble service. Heaven will be a place of loving, selfless service. If it were anything else it would be hell. Everyone will be intent on loving service. As citizens of heaven, therefore, we are to take everything we have and everything we are, with all the rights, rank, position and status that we may think we have achieved in this life, and to use them in selfless service of His people. Remember chapter 2:3-4? *Do nothing from rivalry or conceit, but in humility count others more significant than yourselves. Let each of you look not only to his own interests but also to the interests of others.*

The mindset of heaven is a mindset of purposeful sacrifice

Jesus' self-sacrifice and selfless service is not a noble but ultimately futile gesture – it actually achieves something. The fully-divine One, in His divinity, took on the form of a human; and the perfectly-human One, in His perfection, took on the curse of the cross. That is the point of verse 8 – there is a point to all the suffering: *He humbled himself by becoming obedient to the point of death, even death on a cross.*

It's not that Jesus died simply as a great demonstration
of humility – though He did humble himself.
It's not that Jesus died in the ultimate act of obedience
– though He was obedient.

It's not that Jesus died tragically at the hands of His enemies – though He did surrender Himself to the wicked schemes of His enemies.

It's rather that Jesus deliberately, intentionally, humbly, obediently and purposefully went to the cross. And on the cross, God the Son bore the curse of God the Father so that His citizens, the citizens of heaven, could walk free from God's anger.

This means that the mindset of Christ is the mindset of purposeful self-sacrifice, bearing the sins of His people as He endured the curse of His Father.

In verses 5-9 of Philippians 2, Paul alludes to Isaiah chapter 53, probably the most famous Old Testament passage on the achievement and purpose of the cross. It speaks of the servant or slave of God going obediently to His death as a sheep to the slaughter. The purpose of His death is to carry the punishment and judgment of God for His people's sin: *But he was wounded for our transgressions; he was crushed for our iniquities; upon him was the chastisement that brought us peace, and with his stripes we are healed. All we like sheep have gone astray; we have turned every one to his own way; and the LORD has laid on him the iniquity of us all* (Isa. 53:5-6).

Isaiah uses the language of sin: *transgression* means deliberately wandering from God; *iniquity* means falling short of a goal; *going astray* is surely self-explanatory. He also uses the language of punishment – *He was **wounded**..., he was **crushed**..., the **chastisement** ... was upon him* – and of substitution – it was *for **our** transgression, for **our** iniquities,*

*His chastisement brought **us** peace, **we** are healed, the iniquity of **us all** has been laid on **Him**.*

So at the cross, Jesus, God the Son, stood in our place to absorb all of the anger of God the Father at our failure to give Him His rightful place in our lives. Jesus received God's judgment for us. Jesus showed us both the passionate love of God, as He willingly humbled Himself to be obedient for our sake, and the perfect justice of God. Jesus was fully man and therefore He was able to stand in our place as a perfect human being. But Jesus was also fully God and therefore, as the one who had been sinned against, He was able to carry His own pure and just judgment for our sin.

Can you see why it is important to insist that the selfless slavery of Christ involved a **purposeful** sacrifice?

It would be possible for me to announce to a congregation one Sunday morning that after the service I am going to perform a supremely selfless act. At the end of the service I could go to the back of the church and lay myself out at the threshold for people to walk on as they leave. As they tread on me on the way out, they would have to say: 'What an idiot!' And they'd be right! Ultimately an act like that achieves absolutely nothing. It is as pointless as going to the top of the tallest building in the City of London and throwing oneself off the top, shouting, 'I love you'. Those who say Jesus died simply as **an example** of love for us to follow are claiming nothing more than that His death was a noble, but ultimately meaningless, act which achieved nothing.

The whole of the Biblical witness to the death of Jesus cries out that His death was **purposeful.** His death was a death of **selfless service,** a **purposeful sacrifice.** Through His death our sins and God's wrath are dealt with, and we are then free to become citizens of heaven, pure and blameless, made righteous by Him for membership of God's people, to live to His glory until *the day of Christ Jesus.*

As we begin to think about the application of this, we need to be very careful that we keep the **purpose** of Christian selfless service in view. Paul's desire for his Philippian partners is that they give themselves selflessly for the sake of others just as Jesus did. This is the mindset of heaven; it should be the mindset of the heavenly citizen. But we must be clear that the selfless service of Jesus was directed towards the eternal well-being of His people. This means that our selfless service should be purposefully directed in the same way. We are not being asked simply to engage in meaningless acts of selflessness with no ultimate aim. The goal of our selfless sacrificial service is to be towards the eternal salvation of God's people.

One of the highlights of the year in our church is our annual week of talks. We turn the church into a restaurant and serve dinner, followed by a talk which gives a clear explanation of *the faith of the gospel.* Of course this involves an enormous amount of work – serving as waiters, washing up, setting up and so on. People of all ages and all backgrounds come to the week – usually up to half would not call themselves Christian. One of the joys of the week is to see senior businessmen in their suits washing up and waiting at table as students sit and eat. Selfless, sacrificial service for the sake of the eternal well-being of others.

The (true) story is told of a theological college in Australia in which there was a cash-flow crisis. The college authorities appealed for students to take on the task of cleaning the college. Students signed up voluntarily for every task apart from one – the cleaning of the communal loos. For two or three weeks appeals were made – no one came forward. Yet the loos remained strangely clean. Early one morning, one of the students went down to the basement to find none other than the principal of the college, on his hands and knees, doing the cleaning with a scrubbing brush. Selfless, sacrificial service for the sake of the eternal well-being of others.

Once we are clear about this mindset of Jesus, it will impact on the way we spend our time, how we use our holidays, our use of money as we give to ensure that *the faith of the gospel* is proclaimed around the world. The eternal well-being of God's people will be more important to us than our career advancement or our personal comfort. In churches where there is a genuine understanding of the mindset of heaven, we find people engaged in selfless service for the eternal well-being of others at every level of church life. This mindset transforms homes, it changes and reshapes whole communities.

The mindset of selfless, sacrificial service is the mindset that God vindicates

Jesus is the 'chief citizen' of heaven. Heaven is going to be a place of selfless service. But Paul hasn't quite finished! In verses 9-11 he goes on to show us that God has vindicated Jesus in order to demonstrate to the whole universe that

Jesus' mindset is the mindset of heaven – to the glory of God: *Therefore God has highly exalted him and bestowed on him the name that is above every name, so that at the name of Jesus every knee should bow, in heaven and on earth and under the earth, and every tongue confess that Jesus Christ is Lord, to the glory of God the Father.*

God has given to Jesus an unequalled position; God has given to Jesus an unmatched name; God has given to Jesus a position of universal rule and unchallenged sovereignty – all *to the glory of God the Father.*

At the *day of Christ Jesus*, when He returns, all people everywhere who have ever lived will bow to Jesus, whether or not they currently believe it. Whether they like it or not, Jesus, as promised in Psalm 2:7-8, has taken His place as the Son of God and God will *make the nations his heritage and the ends of the earth his possession.* What God says of Himself in Isaiah 45:23, which Paul quotes here in verses 10-11, is already true of Jesus: *to me every knee shall bow, and every tongue shall swear allegiance.* But, as we have seen, the one to whom we bow will be the glorified one who has shown that at the heart of the character of God is selfless love. As Graham Kendrick puts it: 'This is our God: the Servant King.' He is the Lamb upon the throne.

Did you notice that the tenses in verses 9-11 all speak of something that has happened already? *God **has** highly exalted him. God **has** bestowed on him the name that is above every name. Jesus Christ **is** Lord.* God has already given Jesus this position. Already He is Lord. When He returns, at *the day of Christ Jesus,* every eye will see it. And God has done all this *to the glory of God the Father.*

That last phrase is easy to miss, but it is vital. It is to the glory of God that God gives Jesus this position, because Jesus has demonstrated so perfectly what it means for God to be God. Jesus has shown us the mindset of God – the mindset of selfless service – so that as we look at the exalted Jesus, the Lamb upon the throne, we see in Jesus the perfect, selfless rule of God.

When England won the rugby World Cup in 2001, one of the men in our office changed the screensaver on his computer. He posted as his screensaver a frame-by-frame display of Jonny Wilkinson's winning drop goal. You can imagine that all of us were eager to encourage as many Australian friends as possible into the office for a chat! By posting the screensaver it was as if he were saying, 'now **this** is England! If you want to know what we are really like, here it is!'

Jesus has been given the position and the name that is above every other one. Every knee will bow, every tongue confess that **this** is what God is like – *to the glory of God the Father.*

Once we realize who Jesus is, what Jesus has done, and the supreme position of sovereignty that God the Father has given to God the Son, it should be no surprise that all through the centuries Christians have insisted that Jesus Christ really is Lord. The *faith of the gospel* for which we *strive side by side* demands that we proclaim the facts as they are.

There is no other religious leader who has either made such claims for himself or acted in such a way. Had Moses, Muhammad or, indeed, Paul, made such claims of divinity for themselves, they would have been stoned for blasphemy. The Buddha certainly never offered his life as a sacrificial servant for the sake of his followers. Only Jesus has made such claims for Himself. Only Jesus has given His life for His people in such a way. Only Jesus has been raised from the grave and exalted to such a position. Only in the Christian faith will we find such a glorious view of heaven. The promise of Islam is that the man of God will be rewarded in heaven with seventy-two virgins for his selfish pleasure.[6] It would be hard to imagine a more ghastly picture of self-serving abuse.

For these reasons, Jesus' followers through time and all around the world have insisted that Jesus Christ is Lord and that one day, whether people like it or not and whether they believe it or not, *every knee will bow*, and everyone will surrender their own personal freedom to Him. This is *the faith of the gospel*. Christians must not shift from it.

In Stalin's Russia, as Christians were marched to the Gulags, they proclaimed that Jesus Christ is Lord. In Pol Pot's Cambodia, as Christians were slaughtered in the Killing Fields, they proclaimed that Jesus Christ is Lord. And today in regimes opposed to the gospel – Iran, Sudan, Saudi Arabia, Afghanistan – as they are put to death for their faith, Christians insist that Jesus Christ is God's Supreme Sovereign.

---

[6] The concept of virgins being kept in paradise for believers can be found in surahs 44:54, 52:20, 55:56, 56:22, 78:31-34 (Abdullah Yusuf Ali's translation). The number '72' can be found in Al-Tirmidhi's collection of Muhammad's life and sayings, *Book of Sunan* (volume IV, chapters on 'The Features of Paradise As Described by the Messenger of Allah', chapter 21, 'About the Smallest Reward for the People of Paradise', Hadith 2687) and in Ibn Kathir in his Tafsir (Commentary) of Surah Al-Rahman (55), verse 72.

We too in the West, as we face less hostile but equally resistant secular humanism, must make this proclamation with the mindset of the heavenly citizen. As we serve our colleagues at work and our friends and family at home with this attitude of selfless, sacrificial service, we can be sure that this is the attitude God loves. It brings glory to God as we serve selflessly and sacrificially. As we spend our energy, our reputation, our money and our time for the service of others, God is pleased. For this is the mindset of heaven. It is the mindset that is loved by God, approved by God and vindicated by God.

Questions:

1. Look closely at verses 5-8. What practical steps did Jesus take as a result of His mindset?

2. The language of a servant or slave refers back to Isaiah 53. What does the servant of God do in Isaiah 53 verses 5-6? What does he achieve?

3. In verses 9-11 what is God's response to the mindset of Jesus? Why does God do what He does for Jesus?

4. In verse 5 Paul says that the 'mind' of Jesus is already ours? What does this mean?

5. What then is the attitude or mindset that should be ours as citizens of heaven?

6. What practical things will it mean for us to 'have the mind of Christ'?

FIVE

A Blameless Partnership

Philippians 2:12-18

¹² Therefore, my beloved, as you have always obeyed, so now, not only as in my presence but much more in my absence, work out your own salvation with fear and trembling, ¹³ for it is God who works in you, both to will and to work for his good pleasure.

¹⁴ Do all things without grumbling or questioning, ¹⁵ that you may be blameless and innocent, children of God without blemish in the midst of a crooked and twisted generation, among whom you shine as lights in the world, ¹⁶ holding fast to the word of life, so that in the day of Christ I may be proud that I did not run in vain or labour in vain. ¹⁷ Even if I am to be poured out as a drink offering upon the sacrificial offering of your faith, I am glad and rejoice with you all. ¹⁸ Likewise you also should be glad and rejoice with me.

Several years ago I was offered free membership of a gym before it was built. Sadly, the building project was completed, so I now have to attend the gym! On two or three occasions during the week, you will now find me plodding sedately along a running machine. As I look around, I find myself surrounded by men and women engaged in levels of energetic, committed and strenuous physical activity the like of which I don't think I have witnessed since leaving the army nearly twenty years ago.

In these verses, Paul calls on his gospel partners in Philippi to give a similar level of energetic, committed and strenuous labour as they work out their salvation in obedience to the Lord.

Paul has already told us that the mark of true citizens of heaven, those who are standing firm in their citizenship, is that they *strive side by side for the faith of the gospel* (1:27). Part of this 'togetherstriving' involves sharing the same *mind.* The mindset or attitude that Paul is speaking about is the *mind* of Christ which, as we saw in the last chapter, is one of selfless, sacrificial service for the sake of the eternal well-being of others. Paul has told us that this *mind* is already ours, if we belong to the Lord Jesus. Now Paul says, *work out your own salvation with fear and trembling.* Paul is calling the Philippians to active obedience as they work out their salvation.

The call to dependent activism

The expression 'work out' is an extreme form of the word 'to work'. It means 'to achieve by toil or hard labour'. It speaks, to quote one writer, 'of a continuous, sustained, strenuous effort.'[1] So this is something that anyone in the world of work is only too familiar with. It is the language

---

[1] F. F. Bruce quoted in Peter O'Brien, *Commentary on Philippians,* NIGTC, Eerdmans, p. 279.

of the building site, the trading floor or the production line. But Paul takes this word and applies it to our salvation as we obey the exalted Lord. The wonderful thing is that Paul gives us **two incentives** as he urges us on: He urges us to **dependent activism** because of what God **has made us** (v. 12), and because of what God **is doing in us** (v. 13).

As we look closely at verse 12, it is worth seeing what Paul does **not** say. He does not say we are to *work for our salvation*. Rather he says we are to *work out our salvation*. The assumption is that this salvation is something we have already. Jesus has given Himself selflessly and sacrificially for the sake of His people; as a result, those of us who have accepted the forgiveness of Jesus are on the 'inside'. There is not a hint that it is our hard work which will achieve or earn us a place as God's heavenly citizens.

When I first prepared to speak on this passage, it was during the 2004 Olympic Games in Athens and Kelly Holmes had already won a gold medal running for Great Britain in the 800 metres. Now that she was competing in the 1500 metres with the hope of winning a second gold medal, the language of the athletics commentator, Brendan Foster, changed dramatically. Before she had won the first gold, he would speak about her as a possible medal hope. He said she was full of nerves and hardly expected to win. Indeed, few who saw it will forget the look of shocked surprise on her face when she crossed the line in first place! However, once Kelly Holmes had won the 800 metres, Brendan Foster started to speak of Kelly 'the champion'. He described her as running like a champion, having the confidence of a gold medallist; she was competing like an athlete who had 'proved herself'. Indeed one could see it in her performance. Race by race by race, she began to exude confidence and run with the freedom of someone who was already a champion. She was not running hoping beyond all hopes that she might possibly achieve something. She ran knowing that she was already a champion.

What Paul is saying to the Philippians here is so easy to see, but so hard to remember. As Christians, we already have our salvation. It has been won for us. We are fully qualified citizens of heaven because of what Jesus has done for us. So when Paul says, *'work out your salvation with fear and trembling',* he is not saying that we have to strive in the hope that we might possibly become what we want to be. Rather he is saying we should strive to be what God has made us already.

The *therefore* at the start of verse 12 adds to the sense of assurance and certainty in these verses and, vitally, it helps us to understand what it means to *obey* and to *work out our salvation*. By using the *therefore,* Paul points us back to verses 6-11, reminding us that Jesus, the chief citizen of heaven, made Himself nothing and emptied Himself into the form of a slave. He went to the cross to carry our sin and enable us to be full members of God's heavenly kingdom. So if we trust Jesus, we are full members of God's heavenly kingdom now. Indeed, this kingdom cannot be shaken; it stands for eternity because God has given to Jesus the name that is above all names and every knee will bow to Him and confess His name. *Therefore* we are to *obey* and to *work out our salvation* following Jesus' model of selfless service for the eternal well-being of His people, knowing that we too will be vindicated.

But Paul doesn't leave it there. Having told us to work out our salvation **because of what God has made us,** he goes on in verse 13 to tell us to work out our salvation **because of what God is doing in us:** *work out your own salvation with fear and trembling, for it is God who works in you, both to will and to work for his good pleasure.*

I think this is the emphasis that I have missed when I have looked at this passage in the past. We are not to *work out our salvation with fear and trembling* with a sense that God might suddenly come and take our salvation away. No! We have already seen that *God will bring to completion that which he began in us* (1:6). Rather we are to *work out our salvation with fear and trembling* because of our awareness of the privilege and honour of having God Himself, our Creator, at work within us to *will and to work for his good pleasure.*

Recently I caught the end of a TV programme about the wedding of the daughter of one of the wealthiest landed gentry in England. In fact, my own daughter was watching it and, I fear, picking up all sorts of expensively unhelpful ideas about what a wedding might be like! This earl was in the process of employing a French chef to join his already substantial kitchen staff for the period of the wedding. We watched the chef preparing for his trial meal, his hands trembling as he sent out each course to the earl. Then there was a period of intense anticipation as the chef waited to see whether he was going to be recruited to the team. It was a make-or-break time for his catering career. Then the earl emerged into the kitchen beaming. The job offer was made, and the Frenchman was almost overcome with a sense of the joy and privilege of joining the team and being part of the wedding.

It is in that sense that we are to work out our salvation in fear and trembling. We are to have a sense of the awesome privilege, the immense honour and unique position that is ours. For God Himself is at work within us to *will and to work to his good pleasure.* In one sense, however, we are not like the French chef at all. Although he was part of a great occasion, he was always 'below stairs'. The real action was above, where the earl was enjoying the wedding of his daughter! As we look at verse 13 again, we can see that our position is altogether different. Where is our Lord and Creator at work? ... *for it is God who works **in** you to will and to work for his good pleasure.*

So we are to *work out our salvation* **because of what God has made us** and **because of what God is doing in us.** I love the careful balance of these two verses. I have given them the title **dependent activism.** They avoid the gung-ho self-sufficiency of the hyperactive isolationist, and they also avoid the timid inactivity of the piously passive.

When I was a teenager, one of my screen heroes was Clint Eastwood. I used to love the scenes of Clint riding off into the sunset with his jaw set like flint and his spurs clinking. Many of his best films would start with at least ten minutes of silent action before he even spoke! The self-sufficiency of the isolationist.

There is no such thing in these verses. We are to *work out* our salvation together, with God Himself at work within us. This is our dependent activity, as we seek to obey God in selfless service for the sake of His people.

Early on in my Christian life I was a member of a group that used to sit and wait on the Lord for weeks and months and years before getting on and engaging in any Christian initiative. I fear that we waited, and waited, and waited, and very rarely did anything! But Paul doesn't say here that we are to wait until we feel led to work out our salvation. Nor does he say that we are to wait for the Spirit to come and lead us out. Rather, as we obediently pray and plan and act, we will find that God is already at work within us both to *will* and to *work* His good pleasure. Even as we prayerfully make our plans and put them into action, God is at work to make sure that we plan and do the right things in order to achieve His perfect purposes. This should give us enormous confidence to get on and work out our salvation!

Paul is a great example in this respect. He has spoken a great deal in this letter about contending for *the faith of the gospel*, and told of his own personal ministry in Rome. He will not step back from his outspoken defence of the gospel (1:20), and is already making plans for his ongoing ministry after his trial: *I will remain and continue with you all* (1:25). He has given thanks to God for the Philippians' energetic partnership as they have worked out their salvation (1:3-8). He has prayed for yet more *fruit of righteousness ... to the glory and praise of God* (1:11). Now he wants them to keep on working out their salvation with further prayerful plans for obedient and energetic ministry.

Sometimes the fear of failure can cripple people and prevent them from engaging in risky adventurous service. Sometimes it can hold up a whole church. In the past, I have sat on church councils where one or two people have been almost paralysed from taking a bold and adventurous decision for *the faith of the gospel.* But verse 13 tells us that as we step out in prayerful, dependent and obedient action, God will be at work to guide and energize us in order to ensure that His perfect will is done. With God at work *in* us, even if things don't quite work out the way we envisaged, we cannot fail!

Very shortly after I was asked to lead the church family in which I currently serve, I received a letter from an elderly Christian down on the south coast of England. I don't remember his name nor do I remember the substance of the letter. Just one thing sticks in my mind – the way he finished off his letter: 'have a big vision, brother'! It was a great way to finish an encouraging letter. With God at work within us *to will and to work for his good pleasure,* we can afford to have a 'big vision' as we *work out our salvation with fear and trembling.*

Paul's gospel partners in Philippi faced hostile opposition from the authorities, who were prepared to imprison and punish obedient Christians who confessed Christ's name publicly. It is not hard to see how these two verses would strengthen them as Paul encourages his readers to keep their eyes fixed on the one whom they now serve. These verses speak about our action, but the focus of the verses is on God's activity. He has won our salvation. He is at work in us. We are to fear Him, not man, nor possible consequences. God will achieve His good purpose through us.

Before moving on to the next few verses, it is worth considering how much energetic, committed and strenuous activity we engage in *for the faith of the gospel*. As we seek to obey the One before whom every knee will bow and whose Lordship every tongue will one day confess, do we give *our salvation* the same level of *working out* as we give to other areas of our life – our social life, our holiday plans, our relationships, our mortgage payment or our career development?

Paul calls us to **dependent activism.** But as we engage in this dependently active mission, there is a real danger, which is laid out for us in verses 14-17. It is the danger of dissatisfaction, which can have a very negative effect on our witness.

The danger of dissatisfaction

As we stand together and as we work out our salvation in **dependent activism**, the suffering and hardship of gospel decisions will always bring with them the danger of grumbling and quarrelling amongst us. Paul warns that where there is an atmosphere of grumbling dissatisfaction, there is a real danger that the blazing witness of our heavenly citizenship might be dimmed or even extinguished; it could also endanger our very membership in heaven – if that were possible:

> Do all things without grumbling or questioning, that you may be blameless and innocent, children of God without blemish in the midst of a crooked and twisted generation, among whom you shine as lights in the world, holding fast

> to the word of life, so that in the day of Christ I may be
> proud that I did not run in vain or labour in vain. Even if I
> am to be poured out as a drink offering upon the sacrificial
> offering of your faith, I am glad and rejoice with you all
> (vv. 14-18).

Paul uses Old Testament allusions and imagery to add
weight to his warning and motivate the Philippians to avoid
this danger. The image *shine as lights* is taken straight from
the book of Daniel. In chapter 12:3, Daniel looks forward
to the coming Kingdom of God in which *those who are wise*
(this is Daniel's way of talking about God's people) *shall
shine like the brightness of the sky above; and those who turn
many to righteousness, like the stars for ever and ever.* It's a great
picture isn't it? In Daniel it refers to God's people who will
turn many others to God by their life and witness. This
shows that we have been right to speak in terms of gospel
living and proclamation as we have explored the idea of
working out our salvation. Paul sees his gospel partners
as shining as lights in the world, and uses this image to
motivate the Philippians to continue *holding fast* to the
word of life.

There is a great deal of discussion in the technical
commentaries about this phrase *holding fast.* It appears that
it could mean either 'holding fast' (as in 'holding on to') or
'holding out' (as in 'offering'). The wider context of this
letter suggests 'holding on to', for the Philippians are being
encouraged in this whole section to *stand firm* as citizens
of heaven. This interpretation clearly fits with the rest of
verse 16, where Paul is concerned that they stand firm
until Jesus returns. However, there is plenty to suggest that

Paul could also mean 'holding out'. After all, the Daniel reference occurs in the context of public witness. Also, the phrase *the word of life* (v. 16) suggests an evangelistic meaning in the context of *a crooked and twisted generation*. Furthermore, Paul has been encouraging the Philippians to *strive for the faith of the gospel*, by which he means that they are to proclaim publicly (or 'hold out') the word.

There are strong arguments for both interpretations, and it may be that Paul had both in mind. If that is the case, then the picture is of the Philippians shining like stars in a dark world as they hold on to and hold out the glorious good news of the gospel of Jesus. In order to grasp this picture fully, we need to get away from the bright lights of the town or city. Next time you are in the country and a long way from any lights, take the opportunity to step out of the car or the house and look up into the sky. Those stars, all of them millions of miles away, are visible across the universe.

The world in which we live, by virtue of having rejected the creator, will always be crooked and twisted. That is inevitable and we should never expect anything different. It is a world under God's judgment. But God's *good pleasure* is for his heavenly citizens to shine like stars in the world as we hold on to and hold out God's word. As we do this, we will inevitably live counter-cultural lives in this world, blazing out God's goodness and glory. There is nothing more attractive and nothing more challenging to the world.

The one thing that could spoil all of this, as we saw above, is *grumbling or questioning* (v. 14). Once again there is Old Testament language behind these words. The word *grumbling* could be translated 'murmuring' or 'muttering'. It's the sort of thing that you might get in the school staff room or the hospital ward room when the government has just announced a major new policy that everyone distrusts! In the Old Testament, it is what the Jews did as God led them out of slavery in Egypt and into His promised land. The Jews grew dissatisfied and discontented as the going got tough and as they faced opposition and hardship. They grumbled and complained against God and against God's leader, Moses. Moses tackled the muttering of the Israelites in Exodus 16:8: *the Lord has heard your grumbling that you grumble against him – what are we? Your grumbling is not against us but against the Lord.'*

It is this picture that lies behind our verse 14. Notice that the grumbling in the desert was directed at Moses but was really a complaint against God. The Israelites grew discontented as they journeyed to the promised land. They took their eyes off what God had rescued them from and what God had rescued them for, and they started to long for the days when they were still in slavery in Egypt. This kind of dissatisfaction could all too easily extinguish the blazing witness of the local church as it works out its salvation. An absence of grumbling and quarrelling will enable this gem of a church in Philippi to be blameless and innocent, *children of God without blemish.* Their grateful response of lives given over to *striving side by side for the faith of the gospel* will be a glorious thank offering to God. They will be a blazing witness as they *work out* their salvation. But if they allow grumbling and complaining to creep into their church, the light will be dimmed; they will be full of blame; they will no longer be pure. Paul might even have to say on the day of Christ that *he ran and laboured in vain.*

'Watch out!' says Paul, 'if grumbling and complaining has crept into your church.' Some of us (not me!) will remember the wartime posters: 'Careless talk costs lives'. They were designed to stop people passing on information about what our armed forces were doing. Paul too says in effect: 'Careless talk costs lives'. Grumbling and complaining are in danger of dimming the witness of the local church, of causing a local church to be full of blame, lacking in innocence. There is a danger that Paul would not be able to rejoice in the Philippians in heaven.

It is my great privilege to have had the opportunity to serve God in the church in which I currently work for over eleven years. One of the things that is remarkable about this church family is the lack of grumbling and quarrelling. I frequently thank God for our level of united partnership. But there are 101 things that we could grumble about! No human leader is ever perfect. Some decisions that have been taken were probably wrong. Other decisions have been taken in the wrong way. We can all too easily rub one another up the wrong way. There will be disagreements about the way things should have been done, or could be done. We have often faced opposition and criticism from outside.

Indeed, because the Israelites in the Old Testament grumbled most consistently about their own leaders, I sat down recently and thought about several Christian leaders whom I know well and I thought about the things we could grumble about. The list is so long I couldn't possibly include it in this chapter! Where one is so indecisive that we could grumble about his indecision, another makes decisions all too quickly. One is too consultative, but another isn't consultative enough, even a little dictatorial. One is shy and not a great 'people person'. Another is so gregarious and extrovert that he can't tear himself away from people and get on with the work he should be doing. And so on, and on, and on!

However, the main thing we need to notice here is that, in reality, the grumbling and complaining is a grumbling and complaining against God. It is all too easy for us as Christians to grow dissatisfied as we *strive side by side* and as we face *opponents*.

Paul is the perfect example of how to avoid this **dissatisfaction**. He writes from his prison cell: *Even if I am to be poured out as a drink offering upon the sacrificial offering of your faith, I am glad and rejoice with you all. Likewise you should be glad and rejoice with me* (v. 17). Here Paul uses the sacrificial language of the Old Testament to speak of his and the Philippians' active service. The thank offerings of the Old Testament often took the form of a drink offering (Numbers 28). Paul seems to see his own possible death as such a *drink offering*. He gives thanks that his life, as it is poured out in service of the Philippians, with the accompanying suffering, is only adding to their sacrifice of selfless service lived out in grateful praise. The way to avoid dissatisfaction is not to grumble about suffering for the gospel, but to remember that all our life lived out in selfless service is only a response of gratitude to God for all that He has done.

These verses contain a great challenge to energetic obedience to the Lord. We are to *work out our salvation* as we bow the knee to the Lord Jesus and confess His name. However, there is no room for independent self-sufficiency here. All of our work for the Lord is enabled by Him. Our very salvation comes from Him. It is a **dependent activism.** As we work out our salvation together *striving side by side for the faith of the gospel,* we will be a beacon – like a bright light on a dark night. It is a glorious picture. It is worth asking ourselves whether that expression *work out* is one we would use of our own energetic obedience to the Lord as partners in His gospel work in our local church.

Questions:

1. In verses 12-13, what are the incentives given by Paul to *work out* our salvation?

2. How do verses 9-11 help us to understand what Paul means by *'as you have always obeyed'* in verse 12?

3. In what ways have the incentives of verse 12-13 encouraged you in *working out your salvation?*

4. What do verses 14-17 tell us about God's intended purpose for the local church?

5. What is it that is in danger of jeopardizing the witness of the local church?

6. In what way does Paul's own example illustrate the mindset of heaven?

SIX

Model Partners

Philippians 2:19-30

[19] I hope in the Lord Jesus to send Timothy to you soon, so that I too may be cheered by news of you. [20] For I have no one like him, who will be genuinely concerned for your welfare. [21] They all seek their own interests, not those of Jesus Christ. [22] But you know Timothy's proven worth, how as a son with a father he has served with me in the gospel. [23] I hope therefore to send him just as soon as I see how it will go with me, [24] and I trust in the Lord that shortly I myself will come also.

[25] I have thought it necessary to send to you Epaphroditus my brother and fellow worker and fellow soldier, and your messenger and minister to my need, [26] for he has been longing for you all and has been distressed because you heard that he was ill. [27] Indeed he was ill, near to death. But God had mercy on him, and not only on him but on me also, lest I should have sorrow upon sorrow. [28] I am the more eager to send him, therefore, that you may rejoice at seeing him again, and that I may be less anxious. [29] So receive him in the Lord with all joy, and honour such men, [30] for he nearly died for the work of Christ, risking his life to complete what was lacking in your service to me.

Every Sunday afternoon through the winter, at the Oval cricket ground in London, the ground staff lay on indoor coaching sessions for young boys. Watching the coaches at work is an education. If it is the hook shot that is being taught, then they begin by explaining the theory of the hook shot. After this a pair of the coaching staff lay on a perfect display of this particular shot. Once the display is complete, they send the boys off to practise. Following the practice, the boys come back to the centre again and a further aspect of the hook shot is explained and so on.

The Oval staff are simply using a standard method of instruction that we find in every sphere of life. When we train speakers to give a talk, we speak about **stating the point** up front, then **explaining it**, then **illustrating it**, and finally **applying** it to a particular situation. I am told that presentations in the business world are conducted along the same lines. No doubt teachers use a similar format in their classrooms the world over.

On the surface, the passage we're looking at in this chapter looks little more than a travel itinerary and a statement of diary plans. The Philippians had collected a financial gift for the support of the ministry Paul is currently engaged in from his prison cell, and Epaphroditus has delivered the gift to Paul in Rome (4:16-18), together with news from the church in Philippi. Paul has written this letter to the Philippians and is sending Epaphroditus back to Philippi with it. In due course Paul will send Timothy, in order to check that the letter has been acted upon and to bring news of the outcome of Paul's trial. Finally, Paul himself hopes to visit once he is let out of prison.

This is the sort of stuff of which letters were full back in the days before telephone and e-mail. How else did you communicate your plans to someone several hundred miles away? So why, you might well ask, am I devoting a whole chapter to these travel plans? Indeed, I once set this passage as one of the practice passages for a group of preachers in training. The young man giving the talk on this section of the letter complained that he had been given a passage that was little more than a travel itinerary. 'I would never preach on this in our church,' he said!

However, on examining these verses more closely, we shall find more and more allusions to points Paul has already made in this letter. It seems that these travel plans and descriptions of Timothy and Epaphroditus are deliberately being held up for us as examples or applied models of all that Paul has been teaching the Philippians. Paul has already stated his point, he has explained it, and now he is giving us an illustration of his point by showing how it is worked out in the lives of these well-known gospel friends of the Philippians, Epaphroditus and Timothy.

Paul stated his point in 1:27: *Only behave as citizens worthy of the gospel of Christ, so that whether I come and see you or am absent, I may hear of you that you are standing firm in one spirit, with one mind striving side by side for the faith of the gospel, and not frightened in anything by your opponents.* Those of us who trust in Jesus Christ are citizens of heaven already. We are to live out our citizenship with conduct worthy of a citizen of heaven. The point is made again at the end of this section of the letter in 3:20–4:1: *our citizenship is in heaven ... stand firm thus in the Lord, my beloved.*

So Paul has stated his point. He has then gone on from 1:28 to explain his point. As we strive *side by side for the faith of the gospel* (1:27), we are to do so with the shared mindset of heaven, which is already ours if we are in Christ Jesus. We are to work it out. It is the mindset of purposeful selfless, sacrificial service for the sake of the eternal well-being of others. Jesus perfectly demonstrated this mindset as He made our citizenship of heaven possible through His death on the cross. He did not consider equality with God something to be exploited to His own advantage, but emptied Himself into the form of a slave. He gave Himself sacrificially for the eternal benefit of others so that they could hear the truth of His kingdom and benefit from it. In humility He considered *others more significant* than Himself (2:3).

Having stated and explained his point, Paul now turns to Timothy and Epaphroditus and holds them up as two examples – illustrations of what he has been talking about.

Timothy: his mind affects his looks

Timothy's Christ-like mind affects where his attention is focused and what he is preoccupied with. He has a gospel mind, and this mind affects his whole outlook on life. All through these verses, Paul deliberately echoes these ideas from earlier in the letter. So verse 20, which reads, literally, 'I have no one else like-souled', uses the language of 1:27 and 2:2, where Paul told his gospel partners to be 'single-souled'. Back in 2:4, Paul told the Philippians to *look to the interests of others*, and Paul clearly implies that Timothy models such behaviour when he claims that everyone else *seeks their own interests* (2:21). Similarly, when Paul says in verse 22 that Timothy has *served* with him *as a son with a father,* we are reminded that Jesus took *the form of a servant* (2:7).

This servant-like, selfless attitude which reflects that of Jesus himself, is most clearly illustrated in the language of verse 20, where Timothy is described as being *genuinely concerned* for the welfare of the Philippians. Imagine the circumstances. Epaphroditus came to Rome with the gift from the Philippian believers, and with news of deepening opposition towards the church in Philippi. The result was that Timothy became worried. He was a man who cared deeply about the gospel work in Philippi because he had a heavenly mindset. We can imagine Timothy awake at night, unable to sleep and pacing the corridor. Perhaps his wife comes down in her dressing-gown to find out what is keeping him up and what it is that is bothering him. Finally she manages to prise it out of him – it's those Philippians. They're on his mind; he's worried about them.

Verse 21 is vital because it shows us the source of Timothy's loving concern. If we didn't have this verse it would be all too easy for us to be deeply challenged by Timothy's example without realizing what it is that has caused Timothy to feel this way about the Philippians. We might go away and try to conjure up a similar concern for God's people by gritting our teeth and forcing ourselves into an attitude of loving care. That would miss the point altogether, for it is Timothy's loving concern for the interests of Jesus that energizes his loving concern for the interests of Jesus' people. The verse begins with the word *for* in the Greek : *(For) they all seek their own interests, not those of Jesus Christ.* So Timothy is concerned for the church in Philippi because he is concerned about the interests of Jesus Christ. Such is Timothy's love for Jesus and concern for Jesus' kingdom, that he has been moved to a love and concern for the people of Jesus Christ. We might say the engine of Timothy's love and concern is to be found in his personal love and commitment to the Lord. **Timothy's mind affects his looks.**

So here is what it looks like to have the mind of Christ. It looks like being genuinely concerned and worried about the eternal well-being of God's people. In other words, having the eternal well-being of God's people as our first concern.

Recently I was at supper with some friends in South London. There was another guest there who is an architect in a firm in London. Throughout supper he kept looking down at something on his knees. Only towards the end of the meal did I realize that even as we ate supper together, he was examining his 'blackberry' to check for e-mails – I couldn't believe it! His mind affects his looks all right. He meditates and dwells on the current project, his clients' needs, his own career and reputation.

Timothy has a mind that is so shaped by the selfless love of Jesus, who emptied Himself into the form of a slave for the sake of His people, that he himself is deeply concerned for the well-being of Jesus' people. He does not look to his own interests. He looks to the interests of Jesus. And the interests of Jesus are wrapped up in the interests of Jesus' work and Jesus' people. So Paul could honestly say to the Philippians that Timothy is *genuinely concerned for your welfare* (v. 20) . Notice that Paul makes this point and drives it home by comparing Timothy with all those who surround him in Rome when he declares he has *no one else like him* (v. 20).

We can imagine Paul, in his prison cell asking himself, 'who shall I send? I could send **John** – but his mind is really on his own personal pleasure in this world. He has set his mind on travelling the world in his retirement. It's the only thing he can think about. He spends his life planning the next cruise, the next holiday. It governs his agenda and his finances. **His mind affects his looks** all right, but he hasn't got a gospel mind – he's looking to himself and his interests and not the interests of Jesus.

I could send **Bridget** – but, to be perfectly honest, her mind is on her social plans and, to be blunt, her future prospects. That's all she can think about. Her social calendar, her holiday plans, trips to the gym and the party circuit dominate. All her so-called selfless service is only ever fitted around the other items on her agenda. It's something she squeezes in at the edges, after she has fixed her theatre trips or her party dates. **Her mind affects her looks all right**, but she hasn't got a gospel mind.

I could send **Malcolm** – but his mind is really set on pleasing his boss and on his reputation. He's a partner in a well-known law firm – Fudge-it, Rip-off and Shred – and immensely conscientious. He's desperate to be the best partner in the firm, but is so concerned with having the finest performance figures at the end of the year that he'll never really engage selflessly and sacrificially in gospel ministry for the sake of the eternal well-being of his colleagues. **His mind affects his looks** all right, but he hasn't got a gospel mind. He's looking only to the interests of his immediate boss and his clients.

Or there's **Timothy** – now there's the man to send! He's genuinely concerned and preoccupied with the interests of Jesus. Everybody who knows him recognizes that he has a higher goal than just self-interest or personal preferment. He is genuinely concerned for the eternal well-being of others. So much so, in fact, that he is prepared to risk his rank and reputation, his status and standing for the sake of Jesus' people. His mind affects his diary. His mind affects his cheque book. His mind affects his career plans. His mind affects his social life.

I once worked with a church leader who posed one question of anybody we were thinking of asking to be involved in ministry in the church family: 'who is he/ she serving?' He might just as easily have asked: 'whose interests are they seeking to serve?' It is a good question, isn't it? It goes right to the heart of the matter. Do I have the mind of Christ?

Think about a few members of your local church, or Christian people with whom you are in contact. Ask yourself these searching questions: Am I seeking to pursue the interests of Jesus by selflessly serving these men and women and by being genuinely concerned for them? Is my concern for their spiritual development and growth something that I put *above* my own interests? Does my mind affect my looks?

It's not hard to see how the example of Timothy serves its purpose here in Paul's letter. Paul has been aiming to strengthen his gospel partners. The aim of this whole letter is to develop a church of wholehearted, single-minded gospel partners who are *of the same mind, having the same love, being single-souled and of one mind* (2:2). Here is exhibit A – Timothy – a man with a gospel mind.

Imagine what might happen in our country if every Bible-believing church were to be filled with men and women like Timothy! It's worth praying for, isn't it? But Timothy isn't the only model held up for us.

Epaphroditus: his mind affects his health

Paul goes on in verse 25 to talk about the immediate plan that Epaphroditus should bring this letter to Philippi from Paul in Rome. Notice that Paul chooses his language very carefully indeed; he avoids fanaticism, but he encourages a wholehearted prioritizing of the gospel: *I have thought it necessary to send to you Epaphroditus my brother and fellow worker and fellow soldier, and your messenger and minister to my need, for he has been longing for you all and has been distressed because you heard that he was ill. Indeed he was ill, near to death. But God had mercy on him, and not only on him but on me also, lest I should have sorrow upon sorrow. I am the more eager to send him, therefore, that you may rejoice at seeing him again, and that I may be less anxious. So receive him in the Lord with all joy, and honour such men, for he nearly died for the work of Christ, risking his life to complete what was lacking in your service to me* (vv. 25-30).

Epaphroditus had a job to do, because Paul was in prison. In the first century, a prisoner lived off what relatives and friends provided, so the Philippians had collected a sum of money for Paul's support. It was money devoted to gospel work. Without the money, Paul's ministry of writing and communicating the gospel would have ground to a halt, which is why Paul calls it an act of *service*. In the absence of global banking and automatic transfers, the money had to be carried by courier, and so Epaphroditus was sent with the cash to give to Paul.

In a sense it was really quite a mundane task. Epaphroditus was acting as a courier, a messenger boy. I was reading this passage with a group of businessmen once. The eyes of one man lit up. 'Here is someone I can really relate to,' he said. 'The trouble with Timothy is that he was a bit too high-profile. We know he ended up planting and leading churches. But Epaphroditus is much more my kind of man. He's a gospel gofer!'

Epaphroditus was doing a relatively mundane-looking job for the sake of the gospel, but what he did was vital for the advance of the gospel. Paul needed the money, and Epaphroditus volunteered to be the dispatch rider. This was the equivalent of putting out the chairs for a meeting, offering hospitality to a visiting speaker, running the church accounts, making the coffee or doing the publicity.

Sadly, Epaphroditus got really sick. Paul emphasises the point by mentioning it twice: *he was ill, near to death* (v. 27); *he nearly died for the work of Christ, risking his life to complete what was lacking in your service to me* (v. 30). It's possible that Epaphroditus fell ill on the journey as he sought to deliver the money (*what was lacking* probably refers to the gift that the Philippians were wanting to give to Paul). Because he realized that the money was vital to the ministry in Rome, Epaphroditus put his very life on the line in order to carry through the gospel work he had been given to do – delivering the money.

It's not hard to imagine the scene in a doctor's surgery: 'Look Epaphroditus, you've got a choice here. You are really sick. I can't force you to take a break. But really – you ought to rest up for several months. Or at least go home. For goodness' sake, think of your family, your friends.'

But Epaphroditus was quite clear in his own mind. He had been given a job to do that he alone, at this point, could do! If he failed in doing the job personally, then the advance of the gospel could be set back. Paul wouldn't have the resources he needed and all Paul's ministry in Rome could grind to a halt. So Epaphroditus laid his life on the line.

Now we need to be very careful here. Epaphroditus didn't go out of his way to get sick; he didn't try to make himself ill. Once sick, however, he was prepared to lay his life on the line for the sake of the gospel, because at this point the advance of the gospel depended on it. It is important that we realize that this is not fanaticism. This is wholehearted gospel prioritization. Paul says: 'Here is the mind of Christ.'

Surely that is why Paul describes Epaphroditus the way he does in verse 25 and in verse 29. In verse 25, Paul calls Epaphroditus *brother*, because he is part of the same heavenly family, enjoying the *encouragement* of Christ, the *love* of God, and the *participation* (partnership) of the Spirit (2:1). Paul calls Epaphroditus *fellow worker*, because he is working out his salvation with Paul. And Paul calls Epaphroditus *fellow soldier*, because he has done just what soldiers do – he has put his life on the line for *the work of Christ – the faith of the gospel.* In verse 29, Paul asks the Philippians to *receive him in the Lord with all joy* and instructs them to *honour such men,* because those who put their lives on the line for the sake of the cause for which they are fighting should be received and honoured with all joy.

So here are two models: **Timothy,** who deliberately puts his own interests aside because, with the mind of Christ, he is giving the interests of Jesus top priority, and **Epaphroditus**, who deliberately puts his life on the line because, with the mind of Christ, he is working for the advance of Christ's work.

One of the questions I have had to ask as I have been thinking about Epaphroditus is: Should we qualify what we say about his hard work for the gospel? Might we qualify his example by adding that it would be foolish to overdo our gospel commitment deliberately; or that it would be a mistake not to take sensible holidays or to ignore the advice of our doctors?

The trouble is that Paul doesn't seem to make any such qualifications. He doesn't tell the Philippians to watch out for Epaphroditus when he gets to Philippi because he is temperamentally prone to a little bit of fanaticism and likely even to put his health at risk for the sake of the gospel. He doesn't do a bit of psychological assessment on Epaphroditus, blaming his tendency to over work on a desire to prove himself. He doesn't remind the Philippians of Epaphroditus' slightly delicate constitution. Instead he says: *receive him ... with all joy , and honour such men* (v. 29).

What Epaphroditus did was worthy because it is Christ-like to put your life on the line for the sake of the gospel. But remember, it is not that Epaphroditus went out of his way to get sick, nor did he try to make himself ill. Instead he realized that the task he had been given was absolutely vital for the advance of the gospel. There really was no one else who could do the job at that point in time. So he put his life on the line for the sake of the gospel.

Once again, all of us are familiar with men and women around us who are prepared to take big risks in order to pursue their interests. In the world of business, we frequently come across men or women who are so driven by their desire to get the deal done that they put their health on the line. Some sports people have their minds so focused on achieving their sporting dream that they put their bodies through extraordinarily demanding training regimes. We frequently hear on the news of soldiers in conflicts around the world who are prepared to put their lives on the line because their minds are set on serving their country.

We are not being encouraged here to a driven fanaticism. However, Epaphroditus does cause us to ask questions about our own level of commitment to *the faith of the gospel*. Do **we** have the mind of Christ? *Being found in human form, he humbled himself by becoming obedient to the point of death, even death on the cross* (2:8).

In his excellent collection of sermons on Philippians, Professor Carson tells the story of John G. Paton. Paton was planning to go as a missionary to the South Sea Islands in the nineteenth century. An ageing Christian said to him, 'You'll be eaten by cannibals'. Paton replied, 'Mr Dickson, you are advanced in years now and your own prospect is soon to be laid in the grave, there to be eaten by worms. I confess to you that if I can but live and die serving and honouring the Lord Jesus, it will make little difference to me whether I am eaten by cannibals or worms; and in the Great Day, my resurrection body will arise as fair as yours in the likeness of our risen Redeemer'.[1] His mindset was the mindset of Christ.

Paul has illustrated his point about the *mind* of the gospel partner by showing us Timothy and Epaphroditus. They are the main focus of these verses, but we ought not to leave this chapter without noticing that Paul himself also serves as an illustration here.

Paul: his mind affects his feelings

It might be possible to come to the end of this chapter with a sense of grim determination. We have heard of *the faith of the gospel*, of gospel plans, and of the advance of the gospel in Rome and Philippi. We have been reminded to stand firm together as citizens of heaven, *striving side by side* for the gospel. We have been shown the example of Timothy and Epaphroditus. It might be possible to embark on this kind of gospel ministry in a cold and dispassionate way, as if it were a business project or military campaign to be worked out.

[1] D. A. Carson, *Basics for Believers*, IVP p. 31.

However, to do so would miss *the mind of Christ* altogether. As we look at the example of Paul, we see that his vertical relationship **with Christ** has brought him into a loving, committed, caring and passionate horizontal relationship **with the people of Christ**.

Therefore, as he writes, Paul's mind is full of godly love, care and concern that has affected his feelings: *I thank my God in all my remembrance of you, always in every prayer of mine making my prayer with **joy*** (1:3-4); *I hold you in **my heart*** (1:7); *I **yearn** for you all with the **affection** of Christ* (1:8). He uses affectionate language to address his readers: ***my beloved*** (2:12) and *my brothers, whom I **love and long for**, my joy and crown ... **my beloved*** (4:1). Paul also alludes to the effect of his feelings in his own life: *that I too may be **cheered** by news of you* (2:19); *lest I should have **sorrow upon sorrow*** (2:27); *that I may be less **anxious*** (2:28).

For Paul the gospel work is not simply a project that he happens to be working on, or a problem that he has to sort out; the Philippians and their concerns are not a pain for him to deal with. They are his life, his love, his longing, his care, his concern and his family.

His mind affects his feelings.

Questions:

1. In what ways does Timothy illustrate the *mind of Christ* that Paul has been encouraging in his gospel partners in Philippi? What words/ideas in 2:19-24 have we encountered earlier in this letter?

2. In what ways does Epaphroditus illustrate *the mind of Christ* that Paul has been encouraging in his gospel partners

in Philippi? What ideas in 2:25-30 have we already encountered?

3. In what ways do Timothy and Epaphroditus challenge our levels of genuine and practical concern for the people of God?

4. Skim through the letter, looking particularly at 1:4-5, 7, 8; 2:12, 19, 27; 4:1. How does Paul's gospel mindset affect his feelings? What does this tell us about the way Paul sees his gospel partners?

5. Think of your own sphere of ministry – where is it that God has placed you to *work out your salvation, striving side by side for the faith of the gospel?* Identify one or two deliberate and practical actions that you could take to implement a gospel mindset there after the model of Timothy, Epaphroditus and Paul.

SEVEN

The Key to Staying Safe

Philippians 3:1-11

[1] Finally, my brothers, rejoice in the Lord. To write the same things to you is no trouble to me and is safe for you. [2] Look out for the dogs, look out for the evildoers, look out for those who mutilate the flesh. [3] For we are the real circumcision, who worship by the Spirit of God and glory in Christ Jesus and put no confidence in the flesh – [4] though I myself have reason for confidence in the flesh also. If anyone else thinks he has reason for confidence in the flesh, I have more: [5] circumcised on the eighth day, of the people of Israel, of the tribe of Benjamin, a Hebrew of Hebrews; as to the law, a Pharisee; [6] as to zeal, a persecutor of the church; as to righteousness, under the law blameless. [7] But whatever gain I had, I counted as loss for the sake of Christ. [8] Indeed, I count everything as loss because of the surpassing worth of knowing Christ Jesus my Lord. For his sake I have suffered the loss of all things and count them as rubbish, in order that I may gain Christ [9] and be found in him, not having a righteousness of my own that comes from the law, but that which comes through faith in Christ, the righteousness from God that depends on faith – [10] that I may know him and the power of his resurrection, and may share his sufferings, becoming like him in his death, [11] that by any means possible I may attain the resurrection from the dead.

Several years ago a friend of mine who is a builder sustained severe injuries as he fell from the top of a ladder. In fact, he was at the top of a double ladder that was fully extended. He was rushed to hospital by air ambulance. What virtually nobody knows, to this day, is that the double ladder was perched in the raised bucket of a JCB. Apparently, as the air ambulance sped towards the scene of the accident, various agricultural vehicles were to be seen speeding away from the scene of the accident, fearful of being discovered by the health and safety inspectorate! The frequently maligned health and safety regulations do have some real value when it comes to the practices of some builders!

Paul's concern in Philippians chapter 3 is the spiritual 'health and safety' of his gospel partners in Philippi. The key to this model church remaining *safe* is their ongoing rejoicing in the Lord: *Finally my brothers, rejoice in the Lord. To write the same things to you is no trouble to me and it is **safe** for you.* (3:1). So Paul's aim in writing is that they should be kept safe.

In the background of this chapter is the hostility and opposition that the Philippians are facing as a result of following Jesus, together with the problem of disagreement and rivalry within the congregation. You will remember that the Philippians are *engaged in the same conflict that you saw I had and now hear that I still have* (1:30); they are facing real opposition. Simultaneously there is evidence of potential disunity in Paul's instruction to *do nothing from rivalry or conceit* (2:3). In the face of this double threat to their gospel partnership, Paul is clear that rejoicing in the Lord will keep them safe.

Here, then is the key to the Christian's spiritual health and safety manual. Just as any marriage is preserved as the husband continues to rejoice in his wife 'until death do us part', and just as any business is kept safe as the partners continue to find joy in working together, so the Philippians will be preserved in their faith as they continue to rejoice in the Lord. We are going to find Paul explaining both what it looks like to *rejoice in the Lord*, and giving us reasons why we should continue to *rejoice in the Lord*.

In an age when there is much talk about Christian affections, here is a whole chapter of the New Testament devoted to what it looks like to rejoice in the Lord.

To rejoice in the Lord is to go on making value judgments about the flesh: it is worthless

We can see from verses 7 and 8 that Paul wants us to make a value judgment about what he calls *the flesh*: *whatever gain I had, I counted as loss for the sake of Christ. Indeed, I count everything as loss because of the surpassing worth of knowing Christ Jesus my Lord.* This value judgment that Paul wants us to make is not a one-off event. He wants us to make the judgment and to go on making the judgment. So in verse 7 he says that he **counted** everything as loss, and in verse 8 that he continues to **count** everything as loss. Paul is speaking about a continuing attitude to what he calls *the flesh*. We can see that Paul wants us to consider the flesh as worthless, because in verse 8 the word translated *rubbish* carries the meaning of 'excrement' or 'dung'. Paul counts **everything** as 'dung' in comparison to the *surpassing worth of knowing Christ Jesus my Lord.*

But what is it that Paul is speaking of when he talks about *the flesh?* We are going to discover that Paul is speaking **both** about all human religious effort to make oneself right with God, **and** everything else! Paul considers any form of religion that seeks a right relationship with God in any other way than through Jesus Christ to be excrement in comparison to 'knowing Christ'. As we learn to *rejoice in the Lord*, so we will develop a similar value system to Paul in these matters. This will be *safe for you.*

Paul's aim in verses 1-7 is to inoculate us against works-based religion. We could give this section the title, 'there is no future in works-based religion'. Paul's focus is on *the flesh* and on putting confidence in *the flesh.* He mentions it four times in verses 2-4: *those who mutilate the flesh ... we ... put no confidence in the flesh ... I ... have reason for confidence in the flesh ... confidence in the flesh.*

By using the term *the flesh* in this way, Paul is referring to what we do when we put confidence in our own human efforts to get us into a right relationship with God through our religious works. It refers to what we might say next in a sentence that begins: 'You must accept me, God, because I...'. *Confidence in the flesh* is the confidence we put in our good works to get ourselves into God's good books.

What Paul says in verses 1-7 shows that there is absolutely no future in any rule-based, ritualistic religion involving rites and ceremonies. Even though this kind of thing looks religiously impressive, it is powerless to bring a person into a right relationship with God. Paul has in mind here a group known as 'Judaisers', whom we encounter throughout the New Testament. The Judaisers sought to persuade new Christian converts that in order to be genuinely included and recognized as God's people, they needed to adopt the Jewish religious rituals, keep the Jewish Law, and be circumcised as God's people were in the Old Testament.

Paul uses extraordinarily aggressive and offensive language to describe them in verse 2:

Look out for the dogs. The word for '*dog*' here is the word used for a wild dog scavenging among the filth and dirt in the streets. The Judaisers taught that in order to be pure for worship, God's people had to engage in ritual rites of washing. They washed their pots and pans, their food and themselves. The dog was obviously considered to be ritually filthy – it lived off the filth of human excrement and dirt. Yet Paul describes the Judaisers as *dogs!*

Look out for the evildoers: literally, *evildoers* translates as 'evil workers'. The Judaisers taught that in order to be right with God, God's people had to engage in the 'works of the Law' prescribed in the Old Testament. Yet Paul describes the Judaisers as 'evil workers', the complete opposite of 'law keepers'.

Look out for those who mutilate the flesh: the pagan priests in the Old Testament used to cut themselves in order to show their devotion to God and to try to attract His attention (1 Kings 18:28). The Judaisers taught that in order to be genuinely marked out as God's people, the new Christians should be circumcised, just as God's people were in the Old Testament. Paul describes them as *mutilators of the flesh* – no different than the pagan priests.

This description of the false teachers shows that Paul sees *confidence in the flesh* as being confidence in rituals, rule-keeping and rites of initiation. His point is as blunt as this: 'any religion that places its confidence in the keeping of religious rituals, rules or rites, is unclean, evil and pagan.'

What Paul says negatively in verse 2, he states positively in verse 3: *For we are the real circumcision, who worship by the Spirit of God and glory in Christ Jesus and put no confidence in the flesh.*

The phrase *the real circumcision* means the real people of God, those who really are marked out as belonging to him. Those who glory in Jesus and do not trust in their own religious efforts of ritualistic rule-keeping – they are God's true people. In other words, with the coming of Christ, suddenly all religious ritual, rule-keeping and religious initiation count for nothing.

For Paul to say all of this was no small thing. In verses 4-6 he goes on to show that his own religious pedigree and performance were second to none. It's as though Paul is drawing a profit-and-loss account sheet. The profit column marked *the flesh*, or 'religious effort', is bulging with achievement. Indeed, he holds himself up in these verses as the finest illustration of what it means to *put confidence in the flesh: If anyone else thinks he has reason for confidence in the flesh, I have more: circumcised on the eighth day, of the people of Israel, of the tribe of Benjamin, a Hebrew of Hebrews; as to the law, a Pharisee; as to zeal, a persecutor of the church; as to righteousness, under the law blameless.*

He has the perfect record of religious initiation – he was *circumcised on the eighth day.* He was not only an Israelite, he was *from the tribe of Benjamin* – one of the two faithful, select tribes of Israel. So his **pedigree** was perfect.

Furthermore, Paul had the **performance** to match! He was a meticulous law-keeper; the Pharisees were renowned for their legalistic enthusiasm. He was a zealous advocate of Judaism as he sought to stamp out the Christian faith. He even considered himself blameless before God.

If there was any future in rule-based religion then Paul would still be into it. He used to be into it – big time! Then when he came face to face with Jesus, it was as if he transferred everything in his profit column to the loss column. Now he knows that all of his 'benefits' are in fact worthless in comparison to knowing Christ Jesus.

So Paul considers that a person who *rejoices in the Lord* will make a value judgment about all 'works-based religion'. But we have to ask the question as to why Paul considers this to be *safe* for the Philippians.

The key to why Paul includes this section of the letter lies back in chapter 1:18-30. There he told the Philippians that *it has been granted to you ... to suffer for his sake, engaged in the same conflict that you saw I had and now hear that I still have* (1:29-30). The Philippians were suffering at the hands of jealous Jews and the secular authorities. Following Jesus, therefore, involved them in costly self-sacrificial ministry. We have already seen in earlier chapters that such self-sacrificial service lies at the heart of genuine Christian discipleship. Knowing Jesus and rejoicing in Jesus involves being transformed into a selfless, sacrificial servant – becoming like Him. In the face of such costly ministry, the temptation for the Philippians would always be to step back from genuine Christian discipleship that rejoices in the crucified Lord and to take up a more acceptable form of religion – the kind of religious expression that Paul describes as *putting confidence in the flesh*. If only the Philippians were to accommodate the views of the Judaisers just a little and adopt some of their practices, then the Judaisers would stop persecuting the Philippians and they could all get on with their religious practice in peace and quiet. Paul wants them to be under no illusion – such practices are worthless and, by implication, spiritually dangerous.

So this part of the letter is not designed to be a warning to us about the dangers of making our own church structures and systems into a new form of works-based religion. It is rather a warning against accommodation with those who hate our claims that Jesus alone provides a right relationship with God. When we begin to experience the pain of knowing Jesus and rejoicing in Him – which we will experience as we follow the way of the cross – then many other forms of religious expression will begin to appear attractive. If only we would be less absolute and exclusive in our claims about Jesus. If only we would be more accommodating to those who think that there might be other ways to God than through Jesus alone. If only we would be prepared to engage in ministry alongside those who deny that lifelong heterosexual marriage between two individuals of the opposite sex is the only God-given place for active sexual expression. If only we would agree that seeing Jesus' death on the cross as God's way of satisfying His just anger at our sin was not the primary way of viewing the death of Jesus. If only we would be prepared to reach an accommodation with 'liberal evangelicalism' or 'open evangelicalism' or 'inclusive church'. If only we would do these things, then we would be sure to avoid some of the pain of knowing Jesus – the hostility and opposition would be gone. But Paul wants us to see that every form of religious expression that puts any confidence in the flesh is *rubbish*. As we learn to value these things rightly, so we will be guarded against being lured away from Jesus by them. This will keep us *safe*.

Indeed, Paul goes further than this in verse 8. He doesn't just consider all religious expression apart from that rooted in the crucified Lord to be *rubbish*. He has *suffered the loss of **all things***. He counts ***all things*** as *rubbish, in order that* he *may gain Christ*.

By speaking about *all things* like this, Paul wants us to see that in comparison to knowing Jesus Christ as Lord, **everything** else is rubbish. Of course we may not all be tempted to step back from following Jesus to follow some other form of religious expression. In our culture, when we begin to experience the pain of knowing Jesus and following Him in the way of the cross, it is equally likely that we will be tempted to pursue some alternative goal. Paul wants us to see that *all things* are rubbish in comparison to knowing Jesus Christ as Lord.

Just recently a friend of mine at church gave me a copy of a new magazine called *The Trader*. The edition he gave me cites the 100 top financial traders in the world. It tells us how much each one earns and ranks them alongside their competitors. The magazine is fascinating for its advertising space. In it we find what the top traders consider to be of real value. There are castles being sold in Scotland, complete with helicopter landing sites! What castle is complete without one of those? Watches worth thousands of pounds are advertised: 'You don't simply own a Patek Philippe – you look after it for the next generation.' There are advertisements for what are considered to be the leading schools and centres of education. None of these things is necessarily wrong in and of itself. However, they are the things which our secular, materialistic world would prize above all else. As a Christian starts to experience the cost of knowing Jesus, he or she may well be tempted to value the things that our culture values over and above the joy of knowing Jesus Christ my Lord.

It may not be the trinkets of *The Trader* magazine that you are tempted to place above Jesus. It may be academic qualifications, your image, your reputation, or your social network in your own comfortable circle of friends and family. As we follow Jesus and engage in *striving side by side for the faith of the gospel* (1:27), we may well find these things threatened. Paul wants us to see that in comparison to *knowing Christ Jesus my Lord,* all these things are *rubbish.*

To rejoice in the Lord is to go on making a value judgment about the flesh, and everything else. One commentator puts it like this: 'Paul did not keep on harking back to his past, secretly longing for the things he had lost. Quite the reverse. He regards them as abhorrent.'[1]

So far what Paul says about the way rejoicing in the Lord works out in practice sounds pretty negative. His

---

[1] Peter O'Brien, *Commentary on Philippians*, NIGTC, Eerdmans p. 390.

aim has been to inoculate us against things that might lure us away from Jesus. As we learn to find these things abhorrent, we will be kept close to Jesus. This will be safe for us. However, he has not yet told us why Jesus is so much more valuable than the things he has mentioned in verses 1-8. So in verses 8-11 he goes on to expand on the value of Jesus and what **He** has achieved.

To rejoice in Jesus is to go on seeking Jesus as the only source of present and future hope

As we look at these verses, we shall see that Paul speaks in terms of **a relationship, righteousness** and **resurrection.** It is these three things that make Jesus more valuable than anything the world has to offer. Paul engages in his pursuit of a relationship with Jesus because of what Jesus has secured in the past. What Jesus has secured in the past guarantees everything in the future. Therefore Jesus is more valuable than anything the world has to offer.

Verses 8-10 speak of Paul's **hot pursuit** of a **relationship** with Jesus: *I count everything as loss because of the surpassing worth of knowing Christ Jesus my Lord. For his sake I have suffered the loss of all things and count them as rubbish, in order that I may gain Christ and be found in him, ... that I may know him....*

It seems that to know Christ Jesus as Lord and to be *found* in Him means being prepared not to have a foot in two camps. As Princess Diana famously put it in her television interview, 'no marriage can survive if there are three parties involved.' To be found in Christ means being exclusively devoted to Him. The Church of England marriage service puts it so well: 'will you, x, take y to be your wife? Will you love her, comfort her, and **forsaking all others** be faithful to her until death do you part?' Our relationship with Jesus should be equally exclusive.

So this is Paul's statement of absolute allegiance to Jesus and it is Paul's rejection of all idolatry. It is his intention to seek Jesus with all his heart, all his mind, all his soul and all his strength. But to have a relationship with Jesus and to rejoice in Jesus means to go on engaging in such a single-minded pursuit. Paul uses the present tense to speak of his relationship, and he speaks about an ongoing desire to be found in Jesus in the future: *I count them as rubbish, in order that I may gain Christ and be found in him.* He is not content to rest on past experience in his relationship; he recognizes that there is an ongoing dimension to it.

I was at the wedding of a friend recently where the best man had done some very careful research before his speech. As the groom courted his bride-to-be, he had enlisted the help of her best friend. All the way through the courtship the groom had e-mailed the bride's best friend and discussed what his best 'next move' should be in order to win his bride. However, once engaged, the bride's best friend had turned over the groom's e-mails to the best man. As you can imagine, it made for a hilarious best man's speech, as we were all let in on the secret of the groom's hot pursuit of his bride!

Paul speaks here of a similarly hot pursuit of Jesus. He is so convinced of the value of knowing Jesus that he is continuously concerned to be found in Him and to gain Him. It is an experience that is in tune with the Psalmist:

unite my heart to fear your name (Ps. 86:11); *with my whole heart I seek you ... my soul is consumed with longing for your word* (Ps. 119:10, 20).

But what is it that makes knowing Jesus so valuable? The answer comes in verses 9-11, as Paul goes on to speak of the **righteousness** that Jesus gives. This righteousness secures for Jesus' people the **resurrection from the dead.**

To be made righteous is to be made 'right with God'. It is what happens when God's judgment on the imperfect record of our sinful deeds is paid by Christ – and at the same time the perfect record of His sinless life is credited to us. It is a word taken from the law courts and it means 'to be acquitted' or 'to be declared to be absolutely in the right'. When a person stands on the steps of the Old Bailey after a long trial and announces, 'I am acquitted', they might equally say, 'I am righteous', or 'I am justified'. (The English noun 'righteous' and the English verb 'to justify' derive from the same Greek word. We use two different words because we don't have a verb 'to righteous'.)

I have only once been very close to a person who was facing a serious court case. The individual concerned had done nothing wrong, but a rival in business took him to court on false pretences. For eleven months it was as if life were put on hold as we waited for the case to come to court. The weight of uncertainty and fear that hung over everybody involved and those close to my friend was ghastly. Eventually the case was thrown out of court even before the hearing. You can imagine the sense of delight and joy and celebration when my friend was pronounced 'righteous' or 'justified'. The champagne bottles were opened and it was time to celebrate!

To be declared 'righteous' by God is to be declared to be perfect. It is to have the verdict of the final day of judgment announced today. It is to know for certain that I will be acquitted on that day. More than that, it is to be seen today as one who is innocent of all charges. To be declared 'righteous' is to be seen as one who is perfect in God's sight. This explains the constant sense of joy and rejoicing, thankfulness and praise that Paul experiences from *knowing Christ Jesus my Lord*. He is full of joy and thanks because he knows that in Jesus he is seen by God as perfect, and therefore he can enjoy a full and open relationship with God.

Paul has already explained how this righteousness is made possible in chapter 2:6-8: *He humbled himself by becoming obedient to the point of death, even death on a cross.* We saw in chapter 4 that Paul was alluding here to Isaiah, who had foretold that the 'servant' would be *wounded for our transgressions, crushed for our iniquities,* and that the Lord would lay *on him the iniquity of us all* (Isa. 53:5, 6).

This is why there is such value in *knowing Christ Jesus my Lord,* for as Paul explains in verse 9, *the righteousness from God ... comes through faith in Christ.* It *depends on faith*, and it is *not a righteousness of my own that comes from the law.*

As we trust in Jesus and his finished work on the cross, so we find that our 'debit balance' has been paid by Christ; and that at the same time the 'credit balance' of Christ's sinless life is 'credited to us'.

In the light of the righteousness that Christ alone can offer, nothing could be more valuable than knowing Christ. Anyone who knows anything about the Old Testament Law or anything about themselves will be only too aware of the Law's high standards and of our own constant failure. No amount of ritual or rites of initiation can deal with our lack of righteousness. Through His death on the cross, however, Jesus makes righteousness possible for those who trust in Him.

The great hymn writer Charles Wesley put it brilliantly in the hymn 'And can it be', when he wrote:

> No condemnation now I dread,
> Jesus, and all in him is mine!
> Alive in him, my living head,
> And clothed in righteousness divine.
> Bold I approach the eternal throne,
> And claim the crown through Christ my own.

Wesley's verse helps us to see the ultimate value of the **righteousness** that a **relationship** with Jesus brings. He points us to the future as he writes that we are 'alive in him' and that we will 'claim the crown through Christ'.

As we look closely at verse 9, we can see that the righteousness comes *through faith in Christ,* it comes *from God,* and it *depends on faith.*

At first it seems that Paul is saying the same thing twice when he says that this righteousness comes *through faith in Christ*, and that it *depends on faith.* However it is more likely that the phrase *through faith in Christ* carries the sense of *through faith in the achievements of Christ.*

If that is the case, then Paul is speaking here about the **grounds and the origin** of the righteousness that Jesus has achieved, together with the **means** by which it is received.

The **grounds** of this righteousness are the faithful achievements of Jesus, who *humbled himself by becoming obedient to the point of death, even death on the cross* (2:8). We are back in the realm of the great achievements of Jesus laid out in chapter 2. Where we are faithless, Jesus was faithful. Where we are disobedient, Jesus was obedient. Where our best efforts at righteousness are always only ever flawed, Jesus' righteousness is perfect in every way. He has won righteousness for us by His self-sacrificial death on the cross.

Paul is also speaking about the **origin** of this righteousness. It comes from God, and is a gift, given to those who will trust Him and turn to Jesus.

The **means** by which this righteousness is received is **faith alone** – not by religious works of the flesh. Paul stresses this over and over again, not only in verses 1-7 but also once more here in verse 9: *not having a righteousness of my own that comes from the law.*

Already we should be beginning to see *the surpassing worth of knowing Christ Jesus my* Lord, and why Paul counts *all things as rubbish, in order that I may gain Christ and be found in him.* As we see what Jesus has achieved on the cross, so we will find ourselves delighting in Him. This joyful valuation of Jesus will lead to us longing to be found in Him. Thus we shall be kept safe from wandering away in search of alternative sources of righteousness.

But Paul hasn't finished yet. A **relationship** with Jesus guarantees **a righteousness from God** that secures **the resurrection from the dead.**

In verses 10-11 Paul talks about the resurrection in two slightly different ways. He speaks of the present *power of his resurrection* and he speaks about *the resurrection from the dead.* We shall come back to the first mention of the resurrection in a moment. *The Resurrection from the Dead* is a technical term that refers to final judgment day and to being with Jesus in His perfect new heaven and new earth. We use the term 'heaven' as shorthand to speak of the physical resurrection of all believers to be with Jesus in His perfect new creation. The Resurrection from the Dead is the ultimate goal of our citizenship of heaven (3:20). It is this that makes *knowing Christ Jesus my Lord* to be of *surpassing worth.* A relationship with Jesus brings to us the status of righteousness with God which guarantees for us our final and ultimate Resurrection from the Dead, which means that we shall be with the Lord for ever in His perfect new creation. To know Jesus, to delight in Jesus and find joy in Him, is to rejoice in a present status that guarantees our future state. This is more valuable than anything that this present world has to offer. No 'flesh-based' religion can ever achieve it. Hence Paul speaks of any form of religion, or any expression of Christianity that denies the sin-bearing, wrath-satisfying death of Jesus, as 'excrement'. This is why he looks at all the prizes that this world has to offer and describes them as 'dung' in comparison to knowing Jesus. For only in Jesus is righteousness from God made available and therefore only in Jesus is resurrection from the dead guaranteed. Again, once we grasp what Jesus has achieved, we will delight in Him and we will want to be found in Him. This will keep us safe from all other options that might lead us away from Jesus.

We frequently take funerals and memorial services in our church for men and women who would appear to have had everything that this world has to offer. Our location at the heart of one of the leading financial centres of the world means that there are men and women around us who have been richly rewarded in this world. It always strikes me, as I take a service with the coffin there beside me, or a picture of the dead man or woman on the front of a service sheet, that without Jesus they have nothing. They may have been the envy of all their colleagues. They may have had a career and a CV second to none. But without a relationship with Jesus and righteousness from Him, there is no resurrection to the new creation – only the terror of God's judgment. I took a memorial service recently for a hugely successful middle-aged man. His brother-in-law came up to me afterwards and said: 'he had everything lined up for his retirement. Everything was in place.' But so far as I was aware, he had no relationship with Jesus Christ. The 'everything' was in fact 'nothing'. As he looks back now on all that he held dear in this life and pursued with all his heart and mind and soul and strength, he must realize that all of this is merely *rubbish* in comparison to what would have been his if he had known Christ Jesus as Lord.

Paul's intention here has been to keep the Philippians *safe*. As they face the hostility and opposition alluded to in chapter 1:28-30, so the temptation is there to step away from a wholehearted pursuit of Jesus. But to step away from a relationship with Jesus and seek after anything else, is to pursue something that is of no ultimate value. These things – whether they be *confidence in the flesh* or *all things* – are ultimately of no value when placed alongside the *surpassing worth of knowing Christ Jesus my Lord.* To rejoice in the Lord is *safe for you.*

There is, however, one final aspect to these verses that we have not yet covered.

To rejoice in Jesus is to be a partner in Jesus' sufferings right up to the point of death

As we look one last time at verse 10, we need to notice what the present power of Jesus' resurrection at work in Paul is striving to achieve. Paul says: *that I may know him and the power of his resurrection, and may share in his sufferings, becoming like him in his death.*

For Paul, to know Jesus and to rejoice in Jesus is to share in Jesus' suffering and to become like Jesus *in his death.* Literally, the verse reads 'to co-partner in his suffering and be transformed into his death'. (It's that partnership word again!) As a friend of mine recently put it: Paul's gospel is not a 'prosperity' gospel, it is an 'adversity' gospel.

I first spoke on this passage several years ago at a friend's wedding. I have to confess that it was only as I was about to preach, and as the verses were being read, that I realized I hadn't really understood what Paul means when he speaks here about knowing *the power of his resurrection* in order to *share in his sufferings.* Of course, I had a personal awareness of the power Jesus gives by His Spirit for living the Christian life. But here Paul suggests that a relationship with Jesus, and the righteousness that this brings, will open up to us the power of the risen Jesus in our lives such that we are enabled to be *like him in his death!* The NIV puts it even more strongly: *I want to ... become like him in his death.*

It is only as we begin to plug this passage back into the whole of the letter that these verses make sense. If we refuse to shift from *knowing Jesus* and proclaiming the *righteousness ... which comes through faith in Christ ... not a righteousness of my own that comes from the law* (v. 9), we will inevitably, like Paul, face opposition from those who have altered the message of genuine Christianity and who teach a watered-down alternative. This will mean, in some places at some times, that we have to *become like him in his death.* It was certainly so for Paul in his prison cell as he faced trial. It was true for the Philippians. It is true for people all over the world today.

In our Western culture, we do not face death for holding to the truth of **righteousness** and **resurrection** through a **relationship** with Jesus alone. However, once we start to make plain that all other forms of works-based religion with their rules and rites and rituals are worse than useless in terms of making us acceptable to God, then we will quickly face opposition. If you doubt me on this, try speaking plainly about the futility of Islam as a means of achieving righteousness in your office or amongst your family and friends. The diversity policies of our offices, schools and public bodies are increasingly set up to legislate against anyone who makes the kinds of claims that Christians have made down through the centuries. As we face the opposition that will inevitably come from a culture that is hostile to the Christian faith, we will find ourselves, like Paul, facing a loss of status, reputation, even rank and position. Then we will need to be reminded that all else is 'excrement' in comparison to *knowing Christ Jesus my Lord.*

Indeed, the tangible mark of a relationship with Jesus, according to Paul, is a life characterized by more and more selflessly sacrificial service as we *strive side by side for the faith of the gospel.* This is what it means to have a relationship with Jesus and to rejoice in Jesus as we anticipate the *resurrection from the dead.* It is joyfully to give ourselves selflessly for the sake of others. As the opposition comes, we need to realize that knowing Jesus is of more value than *everything.*

It would be worth sitting down and drawing up a 'profit and loss' analysis of all that we consider to be of value. Paul says: *I count everything as loss.* So put *everything* down – family, friends, career, possessions, holidays, hobbies, achievements and so on. Take some time over it. What does Paul have to say about these things when we compare them to knowing Jesus? Verse 8 has the answer for us.

There is much talk these days in evangelical circles about what it means to have 'affection' for Jesus Christ. People frequently take us back to the great seventeenth-century divines in order to trace for us what it might look like for a person who is emotionally engaged with Jesus. In contrast to much of the sentimentalism that passes for religious experience today, the Puritans of the seventeenth-century uniformly spoke in similar terms to those we have found here in Philippians 3 as they traced out how a genuine engagement or relationship with Jesus should shape up. Paul is seeking to cause us to *rejoice* in Jesus, because he knows that it *is safe* for us to do so (v. 1). As we rejoice in Jesus, so we will be safe, protected from things that will cause us to fall away in times of opposition. The person who delights in Jesus will go on making a value judgment about the flesh, and everything else: it is worthless. The person who delights in Jesus will go on seeking Jesus as the only source of righteousness and resurrection. The person who delights in Jesus will want to partner in Jesus' sufferings right up to the point of death.

Questions:

1. From verses 1-6: what does Paul mean when he talks about *confidence in the flesh?* Why does he have reason for such confidence?

2. Paul's religious performance and pedigree gave him a certain level of acceptance and status amongst the Jewish and Roman establishment. What forms of religious ritual, rule-keeping and rites of initiation are similarly acceptable in our culture?

3. From verses 8-11: what is it about Jesus that causes Paul to reject what he previously counted as *gain?*

4. How does what Paul says about Jesus in verses 9-11 affect his evaluation of what he previously thought to be important? How much of what Paul once considered to be of value does he now consider to be *rubbish* (v. 8)?

5. Can you think why the Philippians might be tempted to turn from rejoicing in Christ alone to a form of religious

rule-keeping, rites of initiation and rituals? (You may need to look back to what we learned about the opposition they were facing from chapter 1:27-30). Why is it *safe* for them to rejoice in Jesus?

6. Draw up two columns, one headed 'profit' the other 'loss'. List everything that you think to be valuable under the loss column. List everything that is found in a relationship with Jesus under the profit column. Which is more valuable?

EIGHT

The Partners' Prize

Philippians 3:12–4:1

¹² **N**ot that I have already obtained this or am already perfect, but I press on to make it my own, because Christ Jesus has made me his own. ¹³ Brothers, I do not consider that I have made it my own. But one thing I do: forgetting what lies behind and straining forward to what lies ahead, ¹⁴ I press on toward the goal for the prize of the upward call of God in Christ Jesus. ¹⁵ Let those of us who are mature think this way, and if in anything you think otherwise, God will reveal that also to you. ¹⁶ Only let us hold true to what we have attained.

¹⁷ Brothers, join in imitating me, and keep your eyes on those who walk according to the example you have in us. ¹⁸ For many, of whom I have often told you and now tell you even with tears, walk as enemies of the cross of Christ. ¹⁹ Their end is destruction, their god is their belly, and they glory in their shame, with minds set on earthly things. ²⁰ But our citizenship is in heaven, and from it we await a Saviour, the Lord Jesus Christ, ²¹ who will transform our lowly body to be like his glorious body, by the power that enables him even to subject all things to himself. ⁴:¹ Therefore, my brothers, whom I love and long for, my joy and crown, stand firm thus in the Lord, my beloved.

A few years ago now I celebrated my fortieth birthday. The staff team at our church very kindly signed a joint birthday card. One of the younger men on the team had drawn a picture of a hill with a stick man on the hill just past the summit, heading down the far side. The stick man had my initials next to it. At the bottom of the picture was the encouraging comment: 'be thankful for eternity'! The implication was not hard to grasp. Once you reach forty you have passed the peak and you are on the way down. Without eternity there would be nothing left to look forward to. He had a point: there comes a time in one's life when one realizes that one is never going to run the 100 metres in under 10 seconds, or pull on an England shirt. There comes a time in one's life when one becomes increasingly conscious of decay and eventually of death itself. My 'friend' on the staff obviously thought I had already begun the downward physical descent to decay, weakness, frailty, indignity and ultimately death! In this chapter we are going to see that a conscious awareness of eternity is a real mark of Christian maturity.

Chapter 3:12 to chapter 4:1 brings the central part of Paul's letter to a conclusion. In his conclusion, Paul makes a final appeal to the Philippians to adopt the mature Christian mindset of heavenly citizens. His request in verses 12-16 is coupled with an encouragement in verses 17-19 that they should emulate his own mature example rather than that of the *many* who had walked away from Christ. He concludes with a closing exhortation to his gospel partners to *stand firm* as those whose *citizenship is in heaven*.

All the way through this section Paul has the eternal perspective in mind. His desire is that the Philippians should have a mature Christian mind. He wants them to understand that the mature Christian's values, goal and direction in life ('what we are on the inside') should be shaped by eternity.

Paul's appeal for the *mature* mindset is easily missed. It is contained in verse 15, where the word *think* is simply the verbal form of the word Paul uses elsewhere in the letter for *the mind*. We could equally translate the verse like this: *let those of us who are mature be **like-minded**, and if in anything you are **minded** otherwise, God will reveal that also to you.*

The spiritually mature Christian will realize that the future lies in the future

We could give this section the title: **we are not there yet!** Paul wants us to see that there is a glorious prize in heaven for the Christian. The mature Christian should be looking forward to it. Paul introduced the idea of an eternal perspective in chapter 3:11: *that by any means possible I may attain the resurrection of the dead.* Now, in two parallel statements in verse 12 and verses 13-14, he reminds the Philippians, and us, that the resurrection of the dead lies in the future: *Not that I have already obtained this or am already perfect* (v. 12); *Brothers, I do not consider that I have made it my own* (v. 13).

Paul repeats this point again in his summary appeal in verses 20-21: *But our citizenship is in heaven, and from it we **await** a Saviour, the Lord Jesus Christ, who will transform our lowly body to be like his glorious body, by the power that enables* *him even to subject all things to himself.* The risen Jesus, who has conquered death and who has been given the position in heaven and on earth that is supreme over all, will one day return and every knee in heaven and on earth will bow to him (2:10). On that day, *the day of Christ Jesus* (1:6, 10; 2:16), he will transform our frail and feeble bodies that are subject to decay and death. He will change our frail flesh that is so full of sin. All the effects of the Fall will be reversed. We will be gloriously sinless and free from deadly decay.

Paul's point here is that this all lies in the future. We have not yet arrived. Therefore part of *knowing Christ Jesus my Lord* (3:8), and rejoicing in him (3:1), is an intense longing for the glorious future of *the resurrection from the dead* (3:11). **The mature Christian will realize that the future is in the future.**

Here, then, is another hallmark of the rejoicing in Jesus that will keep us *safe* (3:1). In chapter 3:10 we saw that *knowing Jesus* was a matter of placing a right value on everything; of pursuing a relationship with Him; and of *becoming like him in his death.* We were able to say then that among the hallmarks of rejoicing in Jesus is joyful, selfless, sacrificial service for the sake of others. Rejoicing in Jesus is not a matter of tingly feelings, but of joining Him in the joy of selfless service. Now Paul has introduced us to another hallmark of rejoicing in Jesus. A genuine, spiritually mature relationship with Jesus will result in a deep longing for the future. If we really do know Christ, then we shall have our eyes fixed on *heaven from which we await a Saviour, the Lord Jesus Christ.*

As we think about Paul himself in the context of his appeal to spiritual maturity, we can see that he is a perfect model of this spiritually mature perspective. In verse 17 he encourages us to imitate him and those like him. Indeed, this future-oriented aspect of his own maturity is evident throughout the letter. In the opening verses he speaks as one who is looking forward to the completion of God's work on *the day of Christ Jesus* (1:6), and his prayer is that the Philippians will be full of *the fruit of righteousness on that day* (1:10). Paul himself is expecting vindication on that day (1:20-1). For Paul, *to live is Christ* but *to die is gain* (1:21). His *desire is to depart and be with Christ*, which he believes will be *far better* (1:23). He knows that on that day *every knee should bow ... and every tongue confess that Jesus Christ is Lord* (2:10-11). He hopes that *in the day of Christ I may be proud that I did not run in vain or labour in vain* (2:16).

Now, says Paul, the spiritually mature Christian will *think this way,* be 'similarly minded' (v. 15), and if the Philippians, or we, are *minded* to think differently, then Paul expects God to change our minds.

I remember when I first spoke on the theme of this passage to a group of over-seventies. I was a young man at the time and it was only as I spoke that I began to realize the glory of the transforming work of Jesus on that last day. As we grow older, we become more and more personally conscious of the reality of decay and death. Parts that once functioned perfectly begin to creak and groan. We find ourselves attending more funerals than weddings. Things start to fall to bits. One wag put it like this:

As you reach middle age you find that you have to sit down to put on your socks. As you approach old age you discover that when you sit down to put on your socks you find yourself asking whether there is anything else you can do while you are down there. Once you have reached old age you find that by the time you have sat down to put on your socks, you've forgotten what you sat down for in the first place!

As we become more conscious of the reality of God's judgment of death in a fallen world, the prospect of Jesus transforming our *lowly body* (v. 21) becomes increasingly wonderful.

But it is not simply a physical transformation and freedom from physical decay that Paul is speaking about here. He also has in mind the frailty of our sinful flesh. One day we will *shine ... like the stars for ever* (Daniel 12:3) as the sinlessly perfect men and women we were meant to be. Every mature Christian, no matter how young or old, will be conscious of their own sinful frailty and should long for that day. As we grow older and see the impact of sin and suffering in our own lives and in the lives and families of our friends, we shall begin to look forward to it more and more.

There is a day set when Jesus Christ, who has paid for sin, who has conquered death and risen triumphant from the grave to be enthroned in heaven, will return and give to His people the perfection of their lowly, humble human state.

All of us who battle now with sin, or who struggle with a sense of inadequacy, fear, failure, insecurity, the 'black dog' of depression or damage done to us by someone in the past, will long for that day. It is the mark of the spiritually mature Christian to yearn for what he has not yet arrived at.

Spiritually mature Christians will invest their present in the future

As a result of realizing that they 'are not there yet', spiritually mature Christians who rejoice in the future will find themselves pressing on in the present. Once again Paul makes the point in the two parallel statements in verses 12 and 13-14: *I press on to make it my own; forgetting what lies behind and straining forward to what lies ahead, I press on towards the goal.* Rather than thinking that he has already attained everything that Christ has to give him, the spiritually mature Christian will have his eyes fixed on *the day of Christ Jesus* as he *awaits a Saviour from heaven* (3:20). This will keep those who are mature pressing on to what lies ahead.

The language of verses 12 and 13 is taken directly from the Olympic arena. The words of verse 13 speak of strenuous and energetic activity. The word for *straining forward* to what lies ahead conjures up a vivid picture of the closing few metres of a race, with the runners reaching for the finishing tape. The picture is of a runner who does not look back over his shoulder but stretches every sinew and muscle as he strains forward to the finishing line. Those of us who have attended a children's sports day will be only too familiar with the instruction not to look back. No matter how wildly the parental fan club is cheering from the sidelines, the instruction to the children is – 'don't shift your gaze from the finishing line'!

By using this imagery, Paul makes it clear that he is not simply urging his partners in Philippi to be vaguely aware of the future. Nor is he asking that they think about the future just once in a while. The present tense of *forgetting what lies behind* suggests that this is something Paul is constantly doing. Mature Christians will have their whole present shaped by the future and will develop a form of amnesia towards the past.

I recently watched a television documentary about a group of Olympic rowers. The programme followed them through the winter as they prepared for the summer games. They were up at 5 a.m. and driving out to the rowing lake in the middle of February. They subjected themselves to a restricted diet. Their training affected their social life, their careers, their relationships – everything. As they left the lake at 8 a.m. on their way to their 'day job', the presenter asked: 'What on earth makes you do all of this? How do you keep going?' Quick as a flash one of the athletes replied, 'the prospect of standing on the podium'. The future affects the present.

Spiritually mature Christians will find themselves similarly focused: *Forgetting what lies behind and straining forward to what lies ahead, I press on towards the goal for the prize of the upward call of God in Christ Jesus* (vv. 13-14).

By way of application, Paul provides us with two possible examples to follow in these verses. The first example is Paul himself and those like him. He urges the Philippians to *join in imitating me, and keep your eyes on those who walk according to the example you have in us* (v. 17).

He has already described what lay behind for him. In his pre-Christian days he invested all his present energies in the present. He had a religious CV to die for. His record of religious good works and ritualistic performance was second to none. He had been through all the religious rites of passage. He was from the jet-set of religious Jewish society. His rank and reputation were unsurpassed. As a Roman citizen in the Roman empire, like his gospel partners in Philippi, he had entry to all the benefits and bonuses that the establishment could offer.

However, once he sided with Christ, he began to live for the future. He *forgot* what lay behind and instead he began to *strain forward* to what lies ahead. He took up the life of selfless, sacrificial service for the sake of the people of Jesus and invested all his present energies in the future Kingdom of Jesus. He had a religious CV to die for but he decided to die for Christ.

Paul's understanding of the future impacted on the present. Once again we can see his example right through the letter. Perhaps it is most clear in his reaction to his coming trial. In chapter 1:20 Paul expressed his absolute conviction that he would be vindicated by Christ on the day of judgment. For that reason Paul was preparing to speak out at his trial with 'full outspokenness' (as *with full courage* can be translated), in spite of the fact that this outspoken witness to Jesus Christ as Lord would increase the likelihood of his conviction and execution. Paul's spiritually mature focus on the future enabled him to invest his present in the future as he gave himself selflessly and sacrificially to the work of Christ. Like an athlete, he was prepared to endure the pain of present suffering and selfless sacrifice, knowing that the crown of heaven awaits him.

However, there were others who evidently started out with Jesus but had ceased to walk with Him. In verse 18 Paul warns us that *many ... walk as enemies of the cross of Christ.* This verse suggests that these people were once at least professing to be part of Christ's people. Precisely what it was that drew them away is debated at length in the technical commentaries. Some suggest that it was the draw of the world and its pleasures, because Paul says that *their god is their belly, they glory in their shame* and that they have *their minds set on earthly things* (v. 19). Greed, ambition and immorality were the bait that lured them from walking with Jesus to walk as enemies of Him, from the selfless, sacrificial service of the cross to self-indulgent hedonism.

Personally, I am more convinced by the suggestion that these *enemies of the cross of Christ* had been influenced by the people Paul was speaking about in verse 2 – the *dogs* and *evildoers* and *the mutilators of the flesh.* By turning from a trust in Jesus alone for righteousness to a concern once again for the rituals about what kind of food they should or should not eat, they were showing that *their god is their belly.* By insisting that circumcision was the way to ensure that they were among the people of God, they were *glorying in their shame,* because their insistence on circumcision as an additional work needed to supplement the finished work of Jesus on the cross was shameful. By thinking that a person could get right with God through keeping the Old Testament moral law, they had *set their minds on earthly things,* for they were constantly worried about whether their behaviour was good enough to get into God's good books rather than rejoicing in the assurance of their citizenship in heaven. All of these things can be summed up in the phrase *they walk as enemies of the cross of Christ.* Instead of sticking to the glorious truth that as Christians we do not have a *righteousness* of our own *that comes from the law, but* one that *comes through faith in Christ, the righteousness from God that depends on faith* (v. 9), these *enemies of the cross* had returned to a more socially acceptable form of works-based religion that denies the unique identity and finished work of Jesus.

Whether it is the pull of the world or the attraction of works-based religion, those who have turned away from Christ have done so because they have failed to keep their eyes fixed on the future. They are not straining forward to the *day of Christ Jesus* with his *prize* of *transforming our lowly body to be like his glorious body* (v. 21). By contrast, the spiritually mature person will have their present priorities and their present goals, aims and ambitions shaped by this future prospect.

Notice what Paul says: all of us *who are mature should think this way* , or 'be like-minded' (v. 15). Paul is not suggesting that mature Christians should contemplate the glory of *the day of Christ Jesus* just once in a while; the imagery of the closing stretches of an Olympic race in verse 14 does not allow for that. Rather every mature Christian who claims any sort of a relationship with Jesus ought to have **their present invested in the future.**

In the City of London where our church is located, there are many business people who genuinely think like that. Of course they have a daily job to do, but it is clear from their priorities – the way they spend their time and use the influence they have at work, or the way they deploy their resources – that they have their eyes fixed on *the day of Christ Jesus*.

One man comes to mind. He makes it a priority to set aside time each week to build relationships with colleagues at work in order to be able to share the gospel with them. He is in one of the most stressful spheres of work in the City, but he is busy investing his present in the future. He knows why the Lord has placed him in the office in which he is working, and he goes about investing in eternity. His ministry has been wonderfully effective. Once every six months he hosts a lunch to which he invites his colleagues and at the lunch he asks a Christian worker to give a short ten-minute address and then answer questions. Numerous men and women in business in the City have heard the good news of Jesus Christ as a result of this individual's 'full outspokenness'.

Precisely what it looks like to have this spiritually mature mindset will be different for each Christian person depending on the personality, situation and gifts of each. It is quite definitely **not** the preserve only of the missionary or of the so-called 'full-time Christian worker' to have their present invested in the future. Paul says, *let those of us who are mature be like-minded*. That refers to all of us – every Christian who is spiritually mature.

For all of us, investing our present in the future will affect the way we spend our time, our money, our weekends and so on. Those who are working from home will have special opportunities within the local community. Those who go out to work will seek opportunities in the workplace to invest in the future. A desire to invest the present in the future will impact on our choice of career. We will want to do a job in which we can maximise our opportunities for investment. It will certainly affect the choice we make about where we live. Rather than choosing a home on the basis of school catchment areas, we will want to live in a place where we can maximise opportunities for selfless service of others. For some this focus that comes from knowing Jesus will result in changes of plans for retirement. For others it might possibly mean substantial career changes.

In our church, we have the privilege of being able to employ a number of young men and women in one-to-two-year 'apprenticeships'. Some of them have given up highly promising careers in order to train for paid Christian work. Some of these individuals have grown up in homes where they were encouraged to invest their present in the present! The goals and ambitions of secular materialism governed their investments. The aim was to get to the best school, in order to get the best results, in order to get to the best university, in order to get the best degrees, in order to get the best job, in order to get the best career and the best pay package, in order to get the best house and the best holidays and so on. The merry-go-round of greedy secular materialism is, of course, dressed up in the respectable language of 'fulfilling one's potential', or 'making the most of the opportunities afforded'. But to be blunt, the bottom line is really – the bottom line. As some of these individuals make decisions to *forget* the prizes of the present in order to *strain forward to what lies ahead,* we regularly hear squeals of protest from those who would rather that they invest their present in the prizes of secular materialism. I thank God that these young men and women are too spiritually mature to *keep their eyes on the example* of those who walk *as enemies of the cross of Christ.*

But what is it that makes sense of the decisions of mature Christians, people who know Jesus, to invest their present in the future?

The spiritually mature Christian knows that the future has been secured by the past.

As we return for the last time to the two parallel statements of verse 12 and 13-14, we can see that Paul gives a reason for the mature mindset that invests the present in the future: *I press on to make it my own* **because** *Christ Jesus has made me his own* (v. 12); *I press on towards the goal for the prize of the upward call of God in Jesus Christ* (v. 14). **Because** Paul has already been grasped hold of by Jesus, he presses on to grasp hold of the *resurrection from the dead* (v. 11). Paul has been called heavenwards by none other than God, so he presses on to reach the heavenly city. He is quite clear that what he is pressing on towards will not elude him. He states the point boldly in verse 16: *only let us hold true to what we* **have attained**.

For the Christian person, citizenship is certain already; there is no doubting our place as a member of Christ's heavenly kingdom. We have been taken hold of by Christ Jesus, who Himself has conquered death, and has risen and ascended as Lord. We have been called by God, who has vindicated Christ Jesus and given Him the name that is above every name; Jesus has been exalted to the highest place. These are the realities of the past and therefore **the future is guaranteed by the past.**

So then, as one who has been called by God and taken hold of by Jesus, the spiritually mature Christian will be focused on the future and will invest in the future knowing that the future is secure. This makes the illustration I used earlier in the chapter of the Olympic rower in training rather inappropriate, for the Olympic rowers have no guarantee of their place on the medal podium. It is altogether uncertain. But the Christian who invests in Christ's kingdom is investing in a rock-solid certainty. The *prize* of verse 14 is in no doubt. The person who has been called by God and made Jesus Christ's own has a future that is guaranteed. As Paul has said already: *God who began a good work in you will bring it to completion at the day of Jesus Christ* (1:6).

Paul's focus is on the future. He wants his gospel partners to *finish the race* and *receive the prize*. That is why he begins chapter 3 the way he does: *Finally, my brothers, rejoice in the Lord. To write the same things to you is no trouble to me and it is safe for you.* Rejoicing in the Lord protects us from being drawn away or distracted from receiving the prize. *It is safe.*

Paul has spelt out what it looks like to enjoy Jesus and to delight in a relationship with him. I suspect that the aspects of *knowing Jesus my Lord* that Paul highlights might be quite different from the things on which we would have expected him to focus. To know Jesus is to delight in the righteousness that He has brought to us. To know Jesus is to find joy in His indwelling resurrection power which enables us to become like Him in His death. To know Jesus is to have every aspect of the present focused on and shaped by His glorious future. To know Jesus is to rejoice in Him. This *is safe for you.*

Questions:

1. Look carefully at the whole of the passage, chapter 3 verse 12 to chapter 4 verse 1. What is it that Paul is looking forward to? What does verse 21 mean?

2. How does Paul's understanding of the future impact on his life in the present?

3. In verses 15-19 Paul points us to two possible models. What are they and why should we follow one and not the other?

4. What does it look like to be spiritually mature?

5. In the whole of chapter 3, Paul has spelled out what it looks like to *know* Jesus and to *rejoice* in Him. What are the marks of someone who has a relationship with Jesus?

6. What major changes to your priorities and the direction of your life does knowing Jesus demand?

NINE

Partners United

Philippians 4:2-9

² I entreat Euodia and I entreat Syntyche to agree in the Lord. ³ Yes, I ask you also, true companion, help these women, who have laboured side by side with me in the gospel together with Clement and the rest of my fellow workers, whose names are in the book of life.

⁴ Rejoice in the Lord always; again I will say, Rejoice. ⁵ Let your reasonableness be known to everyone. The Lord is at hand; ⁶ do not be anxious about anything, but in everything by prayer and supplication with thanksgiving let your requests be made known to God. ⁷ And the peace of God, which surpasses all understanding, will guard your hearts and your minds in Christ Jesus.

⁸ Finally, brothers, whatever is true, whatever is honourable, whatever is just, whatever is pure, whatever is lovely, whatever is commendable, if there is any excellence, if there is anything worthy of praise, think about these things. ⁹ What you have learned and received and heard and seen in me – practise these things, and the God of peace will be with you.

Disunity cripples any organization: no team can stand if there is disagreement and backbiting in the changing-room; no school can stand if there is disloyalty and petty squabbling in the staffroom; no family can stand if there is suppressed anger and sulking around the breakfast table; no church can stand if there is disunity and dysfunction in its relationships.

It seems that both Macedonian churches planted by Paul, in Philippi and Thessalonica, were model churches. However, in both the Christians were facing opposition. In the face of deep hostility and opposition from the world around them, Paul's great concern in Philippi has been that the Christians there should stand **together**, contending side by side as citizens of heaven for the gospel truth. All of this is clear from the key verses of the letter, chapter 1:27-30. The whole of the central section of the letter from 1:27–4:1 is geared towards encouraging the Philippians to stand *firm in one spirit, with one mind striving side by side for the faith of the gospel, and not frightened in anything by your opponents* (1:27-8).

So unity is one of the big underlying themes of the letter as Paul encourages his gospel partners to stand firm. In chapter 2:3-4, Paul has hinted at some disagreement amongst his partners in Philippi: *Do nothing from rivalry or conceit but in humility count others more significant than yourselves. Let each of you look not only to his own interests but also to the interests of others.* He knows that any church beset by backbiting, personal agendas and petty rivalry can never be effective in gospel ministry. Unlike the spin merchants of a political movement, however, Paul is seeking to do far more than simply paper over the cracks of personal disagreement with a few well-chosen soundbites. He is working at the foundations of each individual Christian within the family of the church as he writes to them about their identity. They are citizens of heaven and they need to develop the mindset of the heavenly citizen, which is theirs already if they belong to Christ.

Now, in chapter 4, Paul turns to a detailed application of the teaching of chapters 2 and 3. As he does so, he brings the disagreement out into the open, and his concern is for unity within the church. His appeal for unity is made on the basis of their common mindset (vv. 2-3). The mindset of the heavenly citizen will produce reasonable responses (vv. 4-7), and these responses will come from a detailed daily discipline of dwelling on and practising gospel truth (vv. 8-9).

In his excellent commentary on Philippians, Alec Motyer likens Paul's teaching on the unity of the church to 'an upturned triangle'.[1]

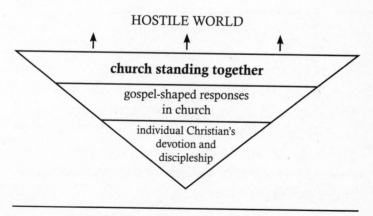

HOSTILE WORLD

church standing together

gospel-shaped responses
in church

individual Christian's
devotion and
discipleship

[1] J. A. Motyer, *The Message of Philippians*, BST, IVP p.106.

The long line at the top is the place where God's people stand together in the face of hostility from the world. This united stand comes from a set of gospel-shaped responses within the heart of the church. These responses are produced by each individual Christian's disciplined devotion and obedient discipleship. This individual discipline and obedience is the point on which the up-turned triangle rests. The aim of these verses, then, is to bring about unity within the church.

Stand firm with your relationships governed by the mind of Christ

A dispute between two women in the church is threatening the Philippians' ability to stand firm together. Paul considers the unity of the Christian brothers and sisters in Philippi to be so vital to their standing and working together in making the gospel known, that he both names the women and enlists the support of his loyal co-worker in Philippi. His public plea to these women to sort out their differences is on the basis of their common identity: *I entreat Euodia and I entreat Syntyche to agree* (literally, *to be of one mind*) *in the Lord* (v. 2).

Anyone who has been a part of any church for more than five minutes can see all too easily what is going on here. The women in the Philippian church were admirable, and had been largely responsible for the setting up of the church. Lydia was the first convert in Philippi, and the slave girl was converted soon after her. Now, however, two of the women have fallen out.

Paul doesn't give us the details of what the disagreement is about. It is almost certainly not a matter of foundational doctrine, otherwise he would, surely, have addressed it directly. It is much more likely in this gem of a church that it concerns a decision that has been taken about the way things are done, or the priorities of the church, or a personal dispute arising from a petty jealousy. The church at Philippi was active and thoroughly involved in gospel work across the Mediterranean. The Christians there supported Paul in much of his work. In a church that is so active and involved, it is all too easy for there to be disagreements over any number of decisions or over the way things are done. In my experience of local church life, I have found that Christians can disagree and fall out about any number of things: how money is spent in ministry; the manner in which decisions have been reached; the style of meetings; the employment of staff; the development of buildings; how children are brought up and educated.

It is not hard to picture Euodia and Syntyche arriving at church on the morning when Epaphroditus turned up with Paul's letter. Perhaps the children had been unusually difficult that morning, and the journey to church a nightmare, so they arrived late and came in through the door together. A couple of years back Euodia and Syntyche had had a bit of a bust-up. It was such a small thing at first – a tiny disagreement over a policy decision within the church – but it had never really got settled. They had once been closely involved together in the work at Philippi, but ever since that bust-up they had drifted apart. There was now an atmosphere of rivalry between them both. Perhaps, as they arrived together, Euodia managed a thin smile but then tactfully steered her family to a slightly distant part of the church so that she didn't have to get too close.

There was quite a buzz about the church that morning. The church's mission partner Epaphroditus was there, and the word was that he had a letter from Paul to the church. What excitement! Euodia settled down to listen.

The first part of the letter was full of news from Paul about his circumstances in prison and the advance of the gospel in Rome. Then there was a tremendous section about citizenship and contending together for the faith of the gospel. There were some extraordinarily pertinent sentences on avoiding selfish ambition, and Euodia quietly hoped that Syntyche had been listening to that bit! Then Paul launched into a description of Jesus and an appeal to work out the salvation he had won for his people. As usual, Paul was deeply concerned that the Philippians should not succumb to false teaching. He made an impassioned appeal to press on until the return of Christ. It was proving to be the most wonderful morning to be in church. And then came the bombshell: *I entreat you Euodia and I entreat you Syntyche to agree in the Lord..*

It's not hard to imagine the shock of being publicly named in this way! But Paul obviously considers the unity of these Christian brothers and sisters to be so vital to their standing together as citizens of heaven that he's not prepared to leave Euodia's and Syntyche's festering sore untreated. He names them, in public, in front of the whole church.

Notice that he doesn't say anything at all about the situation itself. He doesn't say, 'look Euodia ... you're being so petty; or, 'do come on Syntyche ... stop standing on your pride.' What he does is to apply the teaching he has been giving in his letter.

The word he uses for *to agree* is a word he has used over and over again. Verse 2 reads literally: *I entreat Euodia and I entreat Syntyche to have* **one mind** *in the Lord.* We are back in the realm of chapter 2: *complete my joy by being of the same mind, having the same love, being in full accord and of one mind* (v. 2); *have this mind among you which is yours in Christ Jesus* (v. 5).

Paul is making a detailed application of chapter 3:15: *let those of us who are mature be thus minded.* His appeal is not made on the basis of the rights and wrongs of the situation. He simply appeals to Euodia and Syntyche on the basis of who they are. The 'what we are on the inside' mentioned so frequently earlier in this letter (1:27; 2:2, 5; 3:15) has real implications for personal relationships within the church.

The first time I ever spoke on this passage I made out that, like Paul, I was intending to name publicly those within the church who were known to be in disagreement, although it was never really my intention to do so. Unknown to me, there had been a very significant disagreement between two women in that church, and the week before it had blown up. I knew nothing of the incident, or of the disagreement, but I was told afterwards that the two women had sat with a growing sense of alarm and horror as the sermon unfolded!

It may well be that there are disagreements in the church of which you are a part. In any living and active church with lively members who are concerned for the work of the gospel, there are bound to be differences of opinion and disagreements. In one sense it is a sign of life. However, where these differences grow into disputes, Paul considers them to be such a serious threat to the ability of the church to *stand firm in one spirit, striving side by side for the faith of the gospel, and not being frightened in anything by your opponents* (1:27-8) that he is prepared to name those in disagreement publicly. He even calls on his *true companion* (v. 3), who is probably one of his co-workers, maybe even Epaphroditus, to get involved in order to help bring the disagreement to an end.

The way to deal with these disagreements is **not** by way of briefing and counter-briefing, telephone calls and e-mails, snatched conversations in the playground or the supermarket check-out queue. Paul does not encourage these two women to think about the positive aspects of each other's character. Instead he goes right to the heart of the matter as he asks them to remember who they are. He appeals to them on the basis of their *mind.*

If you are aware of anyone within your church with whom you experience rivalry, or with whom you have an unresolved conflict, then it needs to be sorted out. The place to start is with your own *mind.* You need to remind yourself who you are. Consider your own citizenship of heaven. Consider the mind of Christ and his selfless humility: *Have this mind among yourselves, which is yours in Christ Jesus* (2:5). Ponder the debilitating impact that your dispute is having on your own and on your church's ministry. It is time to sort it out.

We are to *stand firm* (1:27) with our relationships governed by the mind of Christ.

Stand firm with your responses guarded by the peace of Christ

Paul is concerned that the reflex responses in Philippi, in every circumstance, with every individual, at every point in time, should be one of joyful, reasonable, prayerful dependence on God.

It is not hard to see how this point relates to the previous one. As we work our way down through the upside-down triangle mentioned in the previous section, it becomes apparent that our relationships are built on our responses. These responses are to be governed by the mind of Christ and guarded by the peace of Christ. The peace of Christ refers to the objective status of 'peace with God' that Christ has won for us by His work on the cross. It is this status of peace with God that enables us to respond rightly in all our relationships, even under pressure.

We shall look at the **responses** first and then the **peace of Christ** from which these responses flow. The responses are responses of rejoicing, reasonable, prayerful dependence.

When Paul urges us to *rejoice in the Lord always; again I will say rejoice* (v. 4), he is not encouraging a shallow and silly jollity in the face of painful suffering. Paul himself has told us he is writing with tears in his eyes. He speaks of the suffering and pain of his imprisonment with real passion and heartfelt pain. Nor when he says *let your reasonableness be known to everyone* (v. 5) is he urging on us a 'roll over and die' approach to opposition. After all, Paul is prepared to say of the false teachers that they are *dogs and evildoers* (3:2) and on a par with pagan idolaters. He tells us in 1:28 that we should *not be frightened of your opponents*. Nor, when he writes *do not be anxious about anything* (v. 6), is he suggesting the state of careless indifference that we find in the 'Hakuna Mutata' ('nothing matters') song in Walt Disney's *The Lion King*. Rather, in each case the **subjective** response of the Christian flows out of the **objective** fact of our identity and what God has done for us as citizens of heaven.

We can see this as we read through verses 4-7 again and ask the question: where do these attitudes of joy, reasonableness and lack of anxiety come from?

> Rejoice in the Lord always; again I will say, rejoice. Let your reasonableness be known to everyone. The Lord is at hand; do not be anxious about anything, but in everything by prayer and supplication with thanksgiving let your requests be made known to God. And the peace of God, which passes all understanding, will guard your hearts and your minds in Christ Jesus.

The **subjective** responses of joy, reasonableness and freedom from worry come from being *in the Lord*. They flow from an awareness of the **objective** truth that *the Lord is at hand* and that *the peace of Christ ... guards us*. In speaking of *the peace of God*, Paul is referring to the peace with God that Jesus has won for us through His work on the cross. This awareness of our position in Christ works itself out in thankful, dependent, prayerful trust in God.

When Paul says *the Lord is at hand,* he must be referring both to the return of the Lord and his immediate presence in the believer. He has been speaking just a few verses earlier of our *awaiting a Saviour from heaven* (3:20). At the same time, he has told us that he *knows* Christ *and the power of his resurrection* (3:10) as a present experience. So the objective truth of the nearness of the Lord fuels the response of joy, reasonableness and freedom from worry.

Once again the central truths of Paul's letter can be applied to us as individuals and as groups of believers. He is urging us together to realize who we are in relation to God and what Jesus Christ has made us. Jesus is near to us, He has won peace with God for us. Therefore as we *stand firm* and *strive side by side for the faith of the gospel* in the face of the hostility of the world, we can bring every situation and every event to Him in prayerful dependence, so that our hearts and minds are guarded by this peace that is ours in Christ.

Paul himself was in prison as he wrote these words. There was no prison inspectorate to ensure high standards of welfare. His trial was a matter of days away and there was no legal aid to ensure he received fair treatment. As Paul faced the possibility of the death penalty, he was writing to the Philippians, who themselves were encountering significant persecution.

These objective truths of the gospel enable us to face every circumstance with a deep confidence that rejoices in the eternal realities which are ours in Christ and can never be removed. They enable us to respond to every situation with reasonableness because we know that the

Lord is near and that we await His salvation from heaven. There is nothing that can remove these things from us. By meditating on them, we will be enabled to entrust our worries and concerns to the Lord and leave them with Him, rather than being plagued by fearful concerns of what might happen.

From time to time over the past eleven years it has been my practice to keep a prayer journal – a record of things I have prayed for. I find it helps me sometimes to be more specific in my prayer requests, and also to concentrate as I pray! As I glance back over the years, I am reminded of any number of different issues that might have caused deep gloom, distracting worry or an irritable response. In the life of any church family there will be painful pastoral issues and practical worries. There have been major political issues within the denomination, staffing complexities, not to mention our own pressing family concerns and the day-to-day relational issues that arise as one contends for the faith of the gospel alongside fellow workers. My own personal testimony is that a deep joy and a sense of freedom from anxiety has flowed from a relationship with the creator God as I have entrusted to Him the concerns and pressures of day-to-day life.

Paul urges us to have our relationships governed by the **mind** of Christ. He has shown us how our responses can be guarded by the **peace** of Christ. Finally he brings us to our own individual discipleship, which is the point of the upturned triangle on which our united stand rests.

Stand firm with a disciplined daily devotion to the Lord

When Paul says, *think about these things* and *practise these things* at the end of verses 8 and 9, the verbs are in the present continuous tense. So Paul's expectation is that we will *think about* and go on thinking about *whatever is true, honourable, just, pure, lovely, commendable, excellent and worthy of praise.* He is saying that as citizens of heaven the affairs, concerns and values of heaven should fill our minds. Once upon a time the Philippians would have filled their minds only with the affairs of their Roman citizenship. No doubt the equivalent in their day of our news columns and media broadcasts would have been the subject of their thoughts. Now, as citizens of heaven, their minds are to have another focus.

This is where radical action is required from all of us. It is only as we fill our **minds** with the affairs of our heavenly citizenship that our **responses** and **relationships** will be shaped by our heavenly mindset. As the upturned triangle diagram illustrates, our responses and relationships are built on our individual disciplined and obedient discipleship, the point on which the upturned triangle rests.

The historian Peter Ackroyd has written what he calls a 'Biography of London'.[2] In a chapter entitled, 'London, loud and everlasting', he points out that the big city has always been a place where voices are constantly calling out and competing for our attention. That is as true today as it has ever been. Friends who come into London from the country often remark on how, as they get nearer to the

---

[2] Peter Ackroyd, *London – the Biography*, Chatto & Windus p.71ff.

centre, they notice the advertising industry clamouring ever more loudly for their attention. Whether it is the advertising hoardings or the television screens, there is intense competition for our thoughts. Paul's point here is that what we focus our attention on will shape our minds.

I had the privilege of having a Christian grandfather, and it was through his witness that I became a Christian. He was a busy farmer in North Norfolk, fully involved in any number of county committees and councils. He also had a busy preaching and teaching schedule in England and overseas. In spite of all the pressing business that he had to attend to, he was always at his desk in his office at 6.15 a.m. with his Bible open *thinking about these things.*

Rather than slumping in front of the television, or spending the first minutes of the day being updated with yet another broadcast from the round-the-clock news industry, what about setting aside some time to *think about these things*? Perhaps our holiday reading might include some planned study of Christian literature so that our *mindset* is being developed in a Christian manner. There are numerous resources now available for personal study in books of the Bible. There are also great Christian 'classics' on key gospel doctrines; studying them is enormously fruitful. I know of several Christian couples who make it their business to carve out time on one evening of the week to listen to a downloadable sermon. I have even met some who download sermons on to their iPods and listen whilst out running or doing the ironing! The key thing is to set manageable and sustainable targets that can be achieved. There are 168 hours in any week. It is worth drawing up a time sheet for ourselves and asking ourselves how many of those hours are spent *thinking about these things* and how many of those hours are spent with our minds being shaped by the world.

As we *think about these things,* so our mindset will be developed in the direction of honour, justice, purity, loveliness, excellence, praiseworthiness and whatever is commendable. A mindset like that will result in **responses** and **relationships** that are *worthy of the gospel of Christ.* A church in which the responses and relationships are governed by the gospel will result in men and women who are committed to strive *side by side for the faith of the gospel* (1:27). The impact of such a church *in the midst of a crooked and twisted generation* (2:15) will be seen and felt far and wide.

Questions:

1. Paul tells us nothing about the nature of Euodia's and Syntyche's disagreement. What does Paul tell us about them? From what we have learned in the rest of the letter, why is it so serious that they are in dispute?

2. When Paul urges Euodia and Syntyche to *agree in the Lord,* the phrase is literally *be like-minded in the Lord.* The idea of *the mind* has come up time and again in the letter. From what we have learned in the rest of the letter, how might their disagreement be settled?

3. In verses 4-6, what is the source of the Philippians' *joy, reasonableness,* and freedom from *anxiety?*

4. What things cause you to lack joy, be unreasonable, or worry? What does the presence of these things do to our

ability to engage in focused partnership in gospel ministry? What is the antidote to these things?

5. Paul tells us to *think about these things.* The tense is present continuous. What prevents us from thinking about these things? How many of the 168 hours in each week are currently given over to thinking about the things listed by Paul? Name the deliberate steps that you need to take in order to change the ratio.

6. Are there any individuals or situations in your church with whom or over which you are in dispute? Why is it so important that you sort it out? What have you learned in this study about how to sort it out? What will you do?

TEN

A Model Partnership

Philippians 4:10-23

[10] I rejoiced in the Lord greatly that now at length you have revived your concern for me. You were indeed concerned for me, but you had no opportunity. [11] Not that I am speaking of being in need, for I have learned in whatever situation I am to be content. [12] I know how to be brought low, and I know how to abound. In any and every circumstance, I have learned the secret of facing plenty and hunger, abundance and need. [13] I can do all things through him who strengthens me.

[14] Yet it was kind of you to share my trouble. [15] And you Philippians yourselves know that in the beginning of the gospel, when I left Macedonia, no church entered into partnership with me in giving and receiving, except you only. [16] Even in Thessalonica you sent me help for my needs once and again. [17] Not that I seek the gift, but I seek the fruit that increases to your credit. [18] I have received full payment, and more. I am well supplied, having received from Epaphroditus the gifts you sent, a fragrant offering, a sacrifice acceptable and pleasing to God. [19] And my God will supply every need of yours according to his riches in glory in Christ Jesus. [20] To our God and Father be glory forever and ever. Amen.

²¹ Greet every saint in Christ Jesus. The brothers who are with me greet you. ²² All the saints greet you, especially those of Caesar's household.

²³ The grace of the Lord Jesus Christ be with your spirit.

Throughout our studies in Philippians we have been reminded that the church in Philippi was a model church. It was a 'dream church' or a 'gem of a church'. Certainly that is the way that Paul refers to the Macedonian churches in his second letter to the Corinthians (2 Cor. 8:1-5). At the same time Paul has unashamedly described himself, and those like him, as model Christian workers. So he writes: *Brothers, join in imitating me, and keep your eyes on those who walk according to the example you have in us* (3:17). In this closing section of the letter we are exposed once again to the **model pastor** and the **model church**.

As we would expect, the closing section draws on many of the ideas that have been running through the letter as Paul encourages the Philippians once again to continue their gospel-centred partnership with gospel workers in spite of the persecution which they are now encountering. Paul writes openly, both about his own concern for his gospel partners in Philippi and about his gratitude for their gospel partnership. We are therefore able to examine this partnership both from the perspective of the model gospel pastor and from the perspective of the model gospel worker.

The model gospel partner
The model gospel worker has an affectionate attachment to the model gospel church. Throughout this letter, we have seen that there is no cold impassive indifference about

Paul. He has been brought into a three-way love affair with the people of God through the love of Jesus for him and for them, and this three-way relationship is evident once again in verse 10: *I rejoiced in the Lord greatly that now at length you have revived your concern for me.*

The Philippians' gift, delivered by Ephaphroditus, demonstrates to Paul that they are still concerned for him. This reminder of their ongoing *concern* (literally their *mind for him* – it's that same word again) is a cause of deep rejoicing for Paul. His rejoicing over the Philippians is a rejoicing *in the Lord.* His vertical relationship with Jesus has produced in him a Christ-like, selfless, loving concern that is horizontally directed towards the people of Jesus' family. Now, as he experiences the love of Jesus for Jesus' people, Paul is like a parent with a child, or like a brother with a sister. He has personal commitment and loving care. The relationship is intense. It is loving, selfless, sacrificial. It is relational at the deepest possible level.

We have seen this **affectionate attachment** for the people of God throughout the letter: *I thank my God in all my remembrance of you ... because of your partnership in the gospel* (1:3); *I hold you in my heart for you are all partakers with me of grace* (1:7); *I yearn for you all with the affection of Christ Jesus* (1:8). Paul's attachment is such that when God's people appear to turn away from Christ, he sheds tears of sadness (3:18).

So gospel work involves people and it involves relationships, three-way relationships of great intensity. Jesus himself is the source of the selfless love demanded by these relationships in gospel work. As the gospel worker grows in his or her grasp of the love of Christ, so there will be a growing love and concern for God's people.

Even though the image of *partnership* is taken from the world of business, the model gospel worker does not set about his work with the same mindset as a business person. Gospel work is much more like raising a family than setting up a production line or analysing figures.

It is possible for a person to begin to lose their love for those amongst whom they are serving. There are times when leading a house group, serving in the Sunday School or being part of a church's welcome or visiting team can become something of a chore. If that is the case, then the key to reviving a right and proper gospel ministry lies in refocusing on the gospel love of Christ. Time set aside to meditate on chapter 2:5-11 should surely revitalize the gospel worker's gospel mind.

Paul, the model gospel worker, has an **affectionate attachment** for the model gospel church. He also has a **dependent independence** from the model gospel church which comes through his relationship with Jesus, for Paul has learned to *do all things **through him** who strengthens me* (v. 13).

Some of the language of verses 11-13 comes from the school of Stoic Greek philosophy. Paul writes: *I have **learned** in whatever situation I am to be **content** ... I have **learned the secret** of facing plenty and hunger....* The word *content* is a word meaning literally 'self-sufficiency', and the idea is borrowed from the world of Classical Stoicism. It is the language of the stiff upper lip and the clenched jaw muscles. But Paul Christianizes the Stoics' self-sufficiency and makes his contentment **dependent.** For the contentment of Paul comes *through Christ who strengthens me,* and it has been *learned.* The concept of 'learning the secret' is suggestive of an initiation. In Christ, Paul has been initiated into the true secret of self-sufficiency, which is **dependence** on the Lord.

Once again we can see the teaching of the whole of the letter underpinning these final few verses. It is the gospel that produces in the model Christian worker a **dependent independence.** Paul's own mind is the mind of Christ that we encountered back in chapter 2:5-11. He has learned the lessons of selfless, sacrificial love for the sake of God's people. He has learned that God will certainly vindicate the selfless love of His people, for selfless, sacrificial love is nothing less than the *mind* of *Christ Jesus* (2:5). So Paul can say: *I know how to be brought low, and I know how to abound. In any and every circumstance, I have **learned** the secret of facing plenty and hunger, abundance and need* (v. 12). In any and every circumstance, Paul is able to draw on the resources and strength of God our Creator, knowing that Christ Himself was *humbled* for a season and became *obedient to death, even death on a cross* (2:8). Similarly, because Christ Himself was *exalted*, Paul, through learning the mind of Christ, is able not only to *be brought low* but also *to abound.*

This is a gloriously liberating lesson for any disciple or gospel worker to learn. For Paul it means that he is not actually dependent on the model gospel church. His dependence on the Lord gives him a very great degree of **independence.**

Of course the model gospel church ought to provide for his keep, and we shall see Paul spell that out in just a moment. But when Paul is working amongst people who do not yet know their gospel responsibilities, or who are unwilling or unable to meet them, that does not stop him doing the work of the gospel. Why? Because he has *learned to be content, in any and every circumstance* (vv. 11, 12). If any church he is working in stops providing his keep, he'll just go and make tents with his hands in order to keep on preaching the gospel! He has been initiated into the secret of true contentment, which is the mindset of cross-shaped, selfless, Christ-like, sacrificial living that ends in suffering and death. It is a mindset which will be vindicated ultimately by God as he exalts those who exhibit it. So the unwillingness or inability of Paul's supporters will never stop him from proclaiming the gospel, and he reminds the Philippians of this in order to demonstrate to them the model gospel worker's mindset of **dependent independence.**

This principle is a vital one for the advance of the gospel. Where established denominations have the resources to provide for the welfare of their paid gospel workers, it is easy for the paid gospel workers to take this provision for granted – indeed, it has been known for some paid workers to become demanding when it comes to housing and other provision.

In the established denominations in England there has been money to support men and women through their full-time training. There has been money to pay salaries and to fund training posts in ministry. Pensions have been provided for paid gospel workers and their widows. There has been a degree of health care available. I have had the enormous privilege of serving a church that is well aware of its gospel responsibilities to provide for its full-time gospel workers and is enormously generous in doing so.

All of this is excellent, and Paul argues elsewhere that the gospel worker is worth his keep.[1] However, it would be enormously detrimental to gospel advance if the mentality were to develop that said, 'I will only engage in gospel work if my needs have been provided for.'

As the established denominations of the West face decline through their failure to preach the gospel, so gospel workers within them will increasingly be brought face to face with the need for **dependent independence**. In many parts of the world, denominational and financial structures such as we have in the West have not yet been established. In such situations the proclamation of the gospel by model gospel workers continues in an atmosphere of constant **dependent independence.** Frequently, the pastor of a church preaches on a Sunday after having tended his land and provided for his family during the week.

Even in our own context, I am aware of young gospel workers who have funded their ministry through part-time work in fast-food restaurants. Others seek part-time employment in order to give two or three days a week of uninterrupted service to the church. This model seems to be far more in line with the experience of Paul and those like him, as they faced the reality of ministry in pioneer situations.

So we have seen that the model gospel worker has an **affectionate attachment** and knows a **dependent**

---

[1] 1 Timothy 5:18; 1 Corinthians 9:3-12

independence. The model gospel worker also seeks a **rich return** for the model gospel church.

What Paul is really after from the model gospel church is not their money, but the fruit of gospel work, which results in credit to their account in heaven and glory to God's name: *not that I seek the gift, but I seek the fruit that increases to your credit* (v. 17). Once again we are reminded of one of the central themes of the letter. Paul's eyes have been fixed on the return of Christ and the glory that will be due to Him when every knee bows and every tongue confesses that *Jesus Christ is Lord, to the glory of God the Father* (2:10). So Paul's concern for the financial giving of the Philippians is not that he, Paul, should be well-fed. Rather, it is that the money they give should result in a bumper harvest of more lives reached and changed for the glory of God. Their selfless, sacrificial financial investment will result in a bumper return for them when they arrive in heaven and find that their financial giving has resulted in their storing up treasure in heaven. This treasure is the fruit of many more people giving glory to God as a result of the Philippians having given so generously.

The language of verse 17 comes from the world of finance. It is as if Paul sees the model gospel church as having a bank account in heaven. Every time the church gives to support the gospel work that Paul is doing, that results in him doing more work, which in turn gives rise to more fruit. That fruit results in their heavenly investment account growing, which means that the model gospel worker is seeking a **rich return** for the model gospel church. Paul wants them to do really well! He is not, of course, saying that they earn a place in heaven through their giving. However, as heavenly citizens, their heavenly treasures increase as they give themselves sacrificially to the advance of gospel ministry. So Paul is delighted to speak of financial matters with them because his eye is on their eternal benefit.

We need to remember that it is God who makes us heavenly citizens. It is all His work and it is all of **grace**. Indeed, Paul tells us elsewhere that it is God who prepares good works for us to do in advance of our doing them (Eph. 2:10). So God made us in the first place, God brought us alive in Christ by **grace**, and God has graciously provided good works for us to walk in as His creatures. Quite incredibly, he then rewards us as we walk in the good works which He has brought us alive to do! It is all of **grace**. Calvin puts it like this: 'For anyone who closely studies the Scriptures, they promise believers not only eternal life, but a special reward for each.'[2] Augustine says: 'God crowns not (our) merits, but his own gifts.'[3]

So Paul, the **model gospel worker,** talks about money. Yes! But as he does so, he has his eye not on his own health plan or his own home comforts. He has his eye on the fruit that will increase to the glory of God. He has **an affectionate attachment** to his gospel partners. He knows a personal **dependent independence** in his ministry. He seeks a **rich return** for those who have invested in his ministry.

---

[2] J. Calvin, *Institutes of the Christian Religion*, Book 3, Chapter 25.
[3] Augustine, *A Treatise on Grace and Free Will*, Chapter 16.

The model gospel church

This closing section also exposes us to the **model gospel church** whose mindful care, responsible wallet and grateful heart are all extended towards the gospel worker and thus towards the advance of God's gospel.

The model gospel church in Philippi has demonstrated a **mindful care** for the gospel worker: *I rejoiced in the Lord greatly that now at length you have revived your concern* (literally *mind*) *for me* (v. 10). You will have noticed that Paul takes the word that we have come across again and again in this letter, 'mind', and uses it in verse 10 to describe their concern for him. The Christ-like, sacrificial and selfless mindset of the citizen of heaven has produced in Philippi a constant care and concern for the model gospel worker. Paul has urged them to *strive side by side ... with one mind* (1:27). He has told them to *have this mind among yourselves, which is yours in Christ Jesus* (2:5). Now he rejoices that this *mind* has been revived towards him.

The word Paul uses for *revived* comes from the world of horticulture. The dictionaries translate it as: 'to cause to grow', or 'to bloom again'. It is used of plants, so the verse could be translated: *I rejoiced in the Lord greatly that now at length your mind has burst forth into fruit again.* It is a picture gardeners will understand well. One of my own great horticultural triumphs is an enormous red azalea that flowers indoors in mid-winter. The plant is kept in the garden until it is brought indoors during late November and put in its pot. Provided one times it just right, the flowering can be engineered to coincide with the three or four weeks either side of Christmas. It produces unjustifiable levels of joy (and rather unseemly pride) in its owner as the buds burst into bloom just before the Christmas celebrations begin! Just as we rejoice in first flowers bursting from their buds again, so Paul rejoices at the fresh flowering of the gospel mind of his gospel partners.

The model gospel church has a mindset so thoroughly impacted by the cross that it has a constant desire and longing to act selflessly and sacrificially towards model gospel ministers and ministries. I have witnessed this being put into practice when visiting mission partners overseas. Frequently they will speak of the loving support, friendship and encouragement of a range of gospel men and women back home. A letter here, a gift there, a visit from someone, a telephone call or an e-mail – all are evidence of gospel concern from gospel people.

To see such genuine, gospel-minded concern bursting into flower is a great joy, but sadly some of us could recount horror stories of churches where there is no such mindful care for those exercising sacrificial ministry in leadership on behalf of the church. As you read this, it is worth asking yourself what you have done, or could do actively, selflessly and sacrificially to show a genuinely Christ-like mind towards those serving in leadership alongside you in your church, or towards other gospel workers further afield with whom you are in partnership. Men and women in gospel leadership can find themselves in positions of great exposure to the hostility and hatred of the world. Paul's joyful thanks (v. 10) captures perfectly the level of gratitude and encouragement that is felt when the **mindful care** of gospel partners is experienced.

The **mindful care** of the Philippian church showed itself in a very practical way. This model gospel church had a **responsible wallet.** The language of verse 15 is the language of the accountant's profit-and-loss ledger: *And you Philippians yourselves know that in the beginning of the gospel, when I left Macedonia, no church entered into partnership with me of giving and receiving, except you only* (v. 15). Paul's gospel partners in Philippi expressed their mindful care by entering into a genuine and proactive partnership with Paul, which involved the sacrificial use of their financial resources. The Philippians exercised their responsibilities in this area by giving financially in order to enable the gospel to go on advancing and expanding elsewhere. This was an appropriate response to all that they had received in the gospel through Paul's ministry among them, which is why Paul uses the language of a bill settled: *I have received full payment, and more* (v. 18).

Paul's concern is not for himself; it is for the ongoing growth of the gospel, the glory of God, and the increased benefit of the Philippians in heaven. However, he is clear that once we have received the gospel through the generous, selfless giving of others, our gospel mind should result in a **mindful care** that results in a **responsible wallet.**

Here, then is a mark of a genuine gospel partnership and a genuine Christ-like mind. It affects our wallets as we give financially to the support of Christian ministry and the proclamation of the gospel. We need to be clear, however, that the motive for this giving is provided by the gospel itself. Christians give out of gratitude, on the basis of grace, in an atmosphere of joy. Giving is not done reluctantly, hoping to twist God's arm into showing favour or giving yet more blessing. Christians give proactively, in a planned way, in order to advance the cause of the gospel. Christians give selflessly and sacrificially as a result of having *this mind among yourselves, which is yours in Christ Jesus* (2:5).

Some, through personal financial circumstances, will be able to give little. Others will be able to give a great deal. In a sense the sum is immaterial. The key issue is the attitude of glad and thankful selfless sacrifice as we *strive side by side for the faith of the gospel.*

Opportunities for giving to gospel work across the world are endless. Many Christians spend time poring over their financial accounts 'on earth'. The pressing daily matters of paying for housing, for other basic needs, for holiday plans (if they can be afforded), and for future needs of family in old age, absorb much emotional energy and thought. The model gospel partner will be conscious of opportunities for investment above and beyond these things.

In the church where I serve, I am aware of many individuals and families who set aside time to draw up a budget for themselves. They think carefully about what they need for the coming twelve months. They look ahead and make wise provision for their family's future. And what they do not need, they give to further the work of the gospel. In Philippi, it seems, the gospel partners went even further. Paul tells us that *they gave according to their means ... and **beyond** their means of their own free will* (2 Cor. 8:3). This was how their gospel mindset blossomed. They made personal sacrifices in order to advance the gospel, even giving up things they might otherwise have needed as they took the path of downward mobility in Christ-like selfless service.

The model gospel church has **a mindful concern** for the model gospel worker. This mindful concern results in a **responsible wallet**, which in turn flows from a **grateful heart.**

Paul speaks of the Philippians' gift as a thank offering in verse 18, and once again he is using terms associated with the Jewish sacrificial system: *I have received full payment, and more. I am well supplied, having received from Epaphroditus the gifts you sent, a fragrant offering, a sacrifice acceptable and pleasing to God.*

There were different types of sacrifice made by priests in the temple. Some were made for the forgiveness of sins and were prescribed by God in order to satisfy His anger at sin and leave His people righteous. However, other sacrifices were thank offerings. These sacrifices were a means by which worshippers could say 'thank you' to God for what He had done for them. The aroma of the sacrifice would rise to God, and as it came from an obedient, grateful heart, it would be pleasing to Him.[4]

The idea first appears in Scripture when Noah steps from the ark and presents a burnt offering with a *pleasing aroma* (Gen. 8:21) as a way of thanking God for his salvation and recognizing that everything comes from God. Of course, it is not that the thank offering in any way 'scores points' with God, or earns air miles to heaven. Noah had already been rescued in the ark; this was his way of thanking God.

---

[4] e.g. Exodus 29:18; Leviticus 3:16

So a thank offering was a means by which a person who already enjoyed God's favour could say thank you. It was made out of a thankful heart, by someone who knew that everything they had came from God.

For the Christian, there is no longer any need for sacrifice to be made for sin. The Christian man or woman has been made *righteous* through the complete and sufficient sacrifice of Christ on the cross. The temple is redundant now. There is no need for an altar, and the sacrificing priesthood is a thing of the past. The Christian man or woman is seen by God as *pure and blameless* (1:10) in Christ Jesus. Indeed, every Christian is now 'a priest' with free and unfettered access to God. The offering of thanks that the Lord delights in is the offering of a whole life of obedient, selfless sacrifice.

As we give ourselves and our resources to God's work, Paul sees our service as a thank offering. All that we are, and all that we are enabled to do, is only possible by His grace. Nonetheless, our grateful response brings real gladness and joy to God. It pleases Him.

We have all seen an illustration of the pleasure that such an offering brings if we have witnessed a small child presenting something to a parent at Christmas. The father or mother is presented with a roughly wrapped package by an eager child. The package is opened and perhaps a mug, luridly painted in primitive form by an enthusiastic child, is revealed. The parent knows that the money to buy the mug came first from them. They are aware that the child only knows how to paint because it was taught first by the parent. Indeed the parent had even given the paints that were used as a gift to the child. Even the wrapping paper and Sellotape used to make the present presentable were bought by the parent. Indeed, the child is only there, only exists, because he (or she) was brought into the world and nourished by the parent. And yet, as the present is given, it brings great joy.

Paul has shown himself to be the model Christian in this regard. He is content to pour out his whole life in selfless service upon the offering of the Philippians' own selfless lives (2:17). The Philippians also are engaged in this acceptable and pleasing sacrifice to God. It involves the whole of their lives, as they too share with Paul in suffering for the sake of Christ, engaging in the same conflict that they saw Paul had and now hear that he still has (1:30).

Their whole life response of sacrificial thanks includes their finances. This model church has given, and given, and given to the work of the gospel. Paul is quite clear that their gift is not only gratefully received by him, but also brings great joy to the Lord as he delights in their gratitude. Paul is also confident that God will continue to supply all that these model gospel partners continue to need.

So Paul's letter concludes. The church in Philippi is a model church. Paul is a model pastor to them. Their relationship is every bit a three-way partnership. He is affectionately attached to them through the gospel. He has learned independence from them through his dependence on God, but as they give to advance the work of the gospel, Paul has a deep desire for their reward in heaven. They, in turn, have a mindful care for Paul. Their gospel minds keep on returning to the advance of the gospel way beyond the boundaries of Philippi and Greece. This care keeps on blossoming in fresh expressions of partnership as they think how they can use their limited resources to further the gospel advance in Rome. Paul makes it clear that this irrepressible gospel mindset that keeps on expressing itself is deeply pleasing to God.

We can only imagine what it might mean for the world and for the glory of God's name if every one of our churches grew to the maturity that Paul wanted for the church in Philippi. Our churches would be *pleasing to the Lord*. We would *shine as lights ... in the midst of a crooked and twisted generation*. As we did so, we would be sure of a similarly hostile response from the world, a world that loves darkness rather than light. However Paul is confident that *my God will supply every need of yours according to his riches in glory in Christ Jesus. To him be the glory for ever and ever. Amen.*

Questions:

1. From these verses, draw up a descriptive profile of Paul, the model gospel pastor.

2. From verses 11-13, where is the *secret* of Paul's contentment to be found?

3. From verse 17, what is it that governs Paul's attitude to the giving of his gospel partners?

4. From these verses, draw up a descriptive profile of the model gospel partners in Philippi.

5. The phrase, *revived your concern*, could equally read 'your mind has blossomed' (see notes). How has the Philippians' gospel mindset burst into flower?

6. From the passage, what is it that has caused this flowering of the Philippians' partnership?

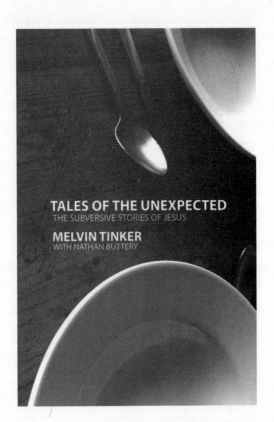

TALES OF THE UNEXPECTED
THE SUBVERSIVE STORIES OF JESUS

MELVIN TINKER
WITH NATHAN BUTTERY

Tales of the Unexpected

The Subversive Stories of Jesus of Nazareth

Melvin Tinker with Nathan Buttery

At Christmas time whilst singing carols about 'gentle Jesus, meek and mild' we can miss that this time-dividing man had an edge about what he had to say. His parables are sometimes not 'nice spiritual stories'.

They capture the imagination, they paint timeless pictures, but they are also more than that. When you read, you get the unnerving sense that through them Jesus can see right through you. They can be unsettling, challenging, able to change you - that the sense of shame and lost-ness that we often feel, may be provided with answers in what he has to say.

The Parable was an unusual form of teaching to Jesus' hearers, the Old Testament has only one main example, yet one third of Jesus' recorded words in the New Testament are parables. If these stories were so important to him, they should also be important to us.

Jesus was a communications genius, his parables convey important spiritual truths – appealing to young and old, rich and poor, educated and non-educated – because they are a not just a story to be understood, they are a spiritual temperature gauge.

Deceptively simple, often taken from everyday Palestinian life; the parables are not just aimed to inform, don't even stop at transforming peoples' lives, but go further; to become part of the means Jesus uses to secure faith in men and women's hearts – they put us in touch with his mind.

Melvin Tinker is the Vicar of St John's Church of England, Newlands, Hull.

ISBN 1-84550-116-0

"THEY COME WITH THE WISDOM, CARE, AND ENCOURAGEMENT
WE NEED TO FOLLOW CHRIST IN THIS CRAZY OLD WORLD"
OS GUINNESS

LETTERS TO A STUDENT

ENCOURAGING WORDS FROM
A CHRISTIAN MENTOR

DONALD J. DREW

Letters to A Student

Encouraging words from a Christian Mentor

Donald Drew

It's a challenging life on campus in the 21st Century. Amongst competing belief systems the only one absent can seem to be evangelical Christianity! Then there are practical concerns and temptations… for parent and student alike it is a testing time.

Some students are fortunate in having a mentor, a Christian with a depth of experience and spiritual wisdom to whom they can turn for help. Donald Drew can be that mentor for you.

'They come with the wisdom, care, and encouragement we need to follow Christ in this crazy old world.'

Os Guinness

'Clear, warm advice on standing firm…each short letter is punchy, well informed and readable.'

Marcus Honeysett, UCCF

'I had his wisdom as my mentor when I was a schoolboy… cuts straight to the core of so many key spiritual issues, yet it does so in a delightfully sympathetic way.'

General Sir Richard Dannatt, British Army

'Aims for Christian integrity without ever being simplistic or legalistic. …radiates an atmosphere of cultured humanity, kindness, hope and respect – which is just what is needed today.

Ranald Macaulay, Cambridge

Dr Donald Drew studied at Cambridge and worked with Francis Schaeffer at L'Abri for six years. He has taught English, spoken in many different countries and is still involved with students and L'Abri.

ISBN 1-85792-866-0

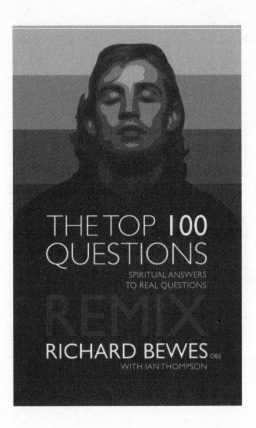

THE TOP **100**
QUESTIONS
SPIRITUAL ANSWERS
TO REAL QUESTIONS

REMIX

RICHARD BEWES OBE
WITH IAN THOMPSON

Top 100 Questions: Remix

Spiritual Answers to real Questions

Richard Bewes OBE with Ian Thompson

As a popular media broadcaster and conference speaker, Richard Bewes often faces tricky questions about the Christian faith. This book collects answers to the top 100 asked by people from all opinions and religious beliefs – remixed for young people.

These are not 'pat' answers to make you feel smug and the questioner seem stupid – they are the sort of thing you could use in a conversation - if only you had thought it out in time!

When you socialise with friends or course mates, living out the Christian faith in the 21st century naturally attracts questions. Here is some instant experience to stop you slapping your head and saying 'if only I'd said that!'.

Top 100 Questions: Remix – it's a great way to answer your mates questions and help you explain why you are a Christian.

'This highly readable book provides direct, clear, concise and relevant answers to questions with which many people struggle.'

Lindsay Brown, IFES

'…gives deeply thought-out, carefully informed answers to many of the questions most troublesome to contemporary humanity.'

Dallas Willard, Professor of Philosophy, USC

'…the accumulated wisdom and illustration from decades of mulling over some very difficult questions - wonderfully distilled down to the key points.'

Rico Tice, Christianity Explored

'…I'm already planning who I could send copies to.'

Peter Maiden, Operation Mobilisation

ISBN 1-84550-191-8

St HELEN'S
MEDIA

St Helen's Bishopsgate in London is committed to serving the wider church by providing gospel-centred resources in both written and spoken format. The St Helen's Media website has a wide range of sermons available (on CD and for MP3 download) by Dick Lucas, William Taylor and many others. Books published by St Helen's include bible study resources on John's gospel and Romans in the *Read, Mark, Learn* series, *Dig Deeper (Tools to unearth the Bible's treasure)* and *Just Love* by Rev Dr Ben Cooper.

Christian Focus Publications

publishes books for all ages

Our mission statement –

STAYING FAITHFUL

In dependence upon God we seek to help make His infallible Word, the Bible, relevant. Our aim is to ensure that the Lord Jesus Christ is presented as the only hope to obtain forgiveness of sin, live a useful life and look forward to heaven with Him.

REACHING OUT

Christ's last command requires us to reach out to our world with His gospel. We seek to help fulfil that by publishing books that point people towards Jesus and help them develop a Christ-like maturity. We aim to equip all levels of readers for life, work, ministry and mission.

Books in our adult range are published in three imprints.

Christian Focus contains popular works including biographies, commentaries, basic doctrine and Christian living. Our children's books are also published in this imprint.

Mentor focuses on books written at a level suitable for Bible College and seminary students, pastors, and other serious readers. The imprint includes commentaries, doctrinal studies, examination of current issues and church history.

Christian Heritage contains classic writings from the past.

Christian Focus Publications Ltd,
Geanies House, Fearn, Ross-shire,
IV20 1TW, Scotland, United Kingdom
info@christianfocus.com
www.christianfocus.com